GO FURTHER

MORE LITERARY APPRECIATIONS OF POWER POP

GO FURTHER

Paul Myers and S. W. Lauden

Rare Bird Books
Los Angeles, Calif.

THIS IS A GENUINE RARE BIRD BOOK

Rare Bird Books
453 South Spring Street, Suite 302
Los Angeles, CA 90013
rarebirdlit.com

Set in Minion Pro
Printed in the United States

10 9 8 7 6 5 4 3 2 1

Publisher's Cataloging-in-Publication data

Names: Myers, Paul, editor. | Lauden, S. W., editor.
Title: Go further : more literary appreciations of power pop /
Paul Myers and S. W. Lauden.
Series: The Mixtape Series.
Description: First Trade Paperback Original Edition. | A Genuine Rare Bird
Book. | New York, NY; Los Angeles, CA: Rare Bird Books, 2021.
Identifiers: ISBN: 9781644281604 (print) | 9781644282076 (epub)
Subjects: LCSH Popular music—United States—History and criticism. |
Popular music—United States—20th century—History and criticism. | Popular
music—1961-1970—History and criticism. | Popular music—1971-1980—
History and criticism. | Popular music—1981-1990—History and criticism.
| Rock music—Appreciation. | BISAC MUSIC / Essays | LITERARY
COLLECTIONS / Essays | MUSIC / Genres & Styles / Pop Vocal

Classification: LCC ML3470 .G6 2021 | DDC 781.6309/047—dc23

Contents

Introduction

Music is limitless, so it only makes sense that once you've gone all the way, the logical next step is to *Go Further.*

In 2019, writers S. W. Lauden and Paul Myers teamed up to curate, compile, edit, and contribute to a literary anthology of music writing and prose that was either focused on or inspired by the oft-maligned rock and roll subgenre known for better or worse as power pop. Tyson Cornell at Rare Bird supported this idea from the start, and the end result, *Go All The Way*, was a fresh compilation of compelling and often personal stories that ranged from pure journalism to personal prose and memoir.

It rocked, and a lot of literate music fans and critics seemed to agree.

As *Go All The Way* became more widely known, other writers reached out to Paul and Steve to express their regret at not being included in the anthology, sharing their desire to be part of any possible second volume. The fantastic response to *Go All The Way* turned the idea of a sequel into a realistic proposition, and the team discovered that not only was there was a lot more to say, new angles from which to deconstruct the broader notion of power pop, but there were still so many great writers out there with diverse experiences and the talent to express it on the printed page.

Like *Go All The Way, Go Further* is an incredibly rich and enlightening collection that will send you seeking out the bands and records you may have missed, while affirming those that you already loved. We won't play favorites with our two editions, but we are thrilled at the consistent quality of our second collection, and we hope you enjoy it as much as we enjoyed putting it together.

Glitter and Glue

By Dave Hill

P OWER POP—WILL WE EVER really understand it? Probably
not. But I, Dave Hill, have at the very least been trying ever
since I was a little kid growing up on the mean streets of suburban
Cleveland back in the seventies and eighties, prime power pop
years any way you slice it.

I'll never remember the name of it, but sometime around
then I watched a made-for-TV movie about a struggling power
pop band (redundant, I know) trying to make it big in their town
while their rock nemesis, a glam outfit whose singer had the good
sense to rip his shirt off (with the help of adoring female fans,
of course) only to reveal he'd had a glittery star on his chest the
whole time (something almost no major chord progression could
possibly compete with in the short term), captured the hearts,
minds, and mullets of everyone that happened to show up at the
mall the day those two bands were scheduled to play on opposite
sides of the second-floor escalator.

And while slapping a glittery star on my chest and having
young, feather-haired beauties rip my clothes off just so I could
be all like, "Check me out—I have a glittery star on my chest and
wasn't exactly crazy about that shirt anyway, so whatevs" held a
certain appeal to me back then and admittedly still does now,

I saw way more of myself in that struggling power pop band, the guys in the plaid shirts with the tobacco-burst guitars and coiled guitar cables who had no intention of disrobing at any point during their set or even after they got home later that night and finished unloading some borrowed station wagon.

Looking back on it now, I don't think it was that dejected power pop band's seemingly mild-mannered and innocent ways or their feel-good approach to rock that I immediately identified with. More likely, it was their sense of longing and almost certain despair of knowing that we live in a world where the noble act of wearing your heart on your sleeve is so often and easily overshadowed by a few bucks' worth of glitter and glue, no doubt bought on a whim with whatever money was left after loading up on fast food, cheap beer, and smokes.

And to me, that's the thing about power pop—while it's dismissed—sometimes even by its biggest fans—as carefree, whimsical, and sugary sweet, the fact of the matter is it's both serious business and a dangerous, dangerous game where people often get hurt. From the most dedicated of power pop musicians to the most casual of power pop fans, we are all Icarus, strapping on our waxen wings, fully intent on flying too close to the sun in search of that perfect combination of words and melody that brings a tingle to the spine, a tear to the eye, or even—let's be honest—a hand to the pants. Sure, it all works out just often enough to keep us coming back for more again and again, but the fact is that power pop casualties far outweigh the triumphs and, more often than not, we come crashing to the ground, a bloodied, swollen, and, not least of all, feather-riddled mess at the hands of an open G to D played one too many times while that Em7 sits at home all alone, the shy and weird yet stunningly beautiful girl who never got asked to the prom because we were all too afraid to ask. Worst of all with regard to power pop (and with the risk of veering too far into the morbid), the luckiest of the bunch seem to get it the worst in the end, from Chris Bell to half of Badfinger to, perhaps most disturbingly of all, 2020 Eric Carmen.

I don't dare try to make sense of power pop's personal misfortunes, but as far as the music itself goes, it all, like most things in life, goes back to the Beatles, who are entirely to blame for introducing perfect pop rock into the world in the first place. Making matters worse, they dressed like mere mortals, at first anyway, to fool us into thinking they weren't gods but regular folk just like everybody else, which, in turn, caused us regular folk to think we could be the Beatles too.

And not only could we not be the Beatles, but we got way too greedy when we even tried.

Sure, we learned the descending guitar melody from "She Loves You," which was, of course, great. But then we had the temerity to think we could make the whole thing even better by adding an extra "yeah!" Next thing you know, we're getting rid of the whole "she loves you" part and replacing it with just a bunch more "yeahs!" like some kid at a birthday party who wanders away from the cake on the dining room table straight into the kitchen to gorge himself on leftover frosting while no one is watching until he pukes everywhere.

My point, of course, is that most of the time when it comes to power pop, things go horribly wrong and, next thing you know, we're lying in the fetal position in the backseat of a Buick with fruit punch–stained lips as our mom drives us back home in silence, her lit Pall Mall dangling just inches from our soft, soft skin, threatening to scar us for life. But every so often, it goes absolutely right, a diamond reveals itself in the manure, and we get a "September Gurls," a "Come On, Come On," a "Baby Blue," or, yes, even a "Go All the Way."

And that's what keeps us coming back for more.

You probably saw this coming, but I sing and play guitar in my own power pop band, just like those guys I saw in that movie all those years ago. We're called Valley Lodge and, like the vast majority of power pop bands past and present, most people have never heard of us. Even so, millions of people have at least heard our music because we had the good fortune of having our song "Go" be chosen as the theme song to HBO's *Last Week Tonight with John Oliver*, something for which I am eternally grateful and, at least once a week as I pretend it's no big deal at all, extremely proud.

I still remember writing the skeleton of the song. My band, in keeping with the ideals of the power pop lifestyle, had just returned from our very first (and, at least as of this writing, last) tour of Japan. I lay in bed one night around 4:00 a.m., sleepless as a result of both the buzz and brutal jetlag that comes with chasing *Live at Budokan* dreams, when I tried to imagine a sound that might summarize everything my bandmates and I had just experienced in between stops at JFK—from recklessly devoured airplane sushi to giggling geishas politely obliging our photo requests; from street-side vending machines selling the unspeakable to near-stoic audience members who suddenly came to life at the first downbeat and knew all the words seemingly better than I did; from our tour manager growing increasingly annoyed at me for loudly repeating phrases from a discounted English-to-Japanese handbook in the back of our van; to the doorman at a Japanese-only strip club surprised to hear me tell him he was "a fantastic dancer" for no apparent reason at all. I thought of all these things and more, when suddenly, as power pop fugue states tend to go, a drumbeat, guitar melody, and countermelody popped into my head all at once. I grabbed my phone and mumbled the whole mess into a four-track simulator I'd recently downloaded before eventually drifting off to sleep, satisfied with the knowledge that I might be onto something that maybe, just maybe, didn't suck.

Over the next few days, I fleshed things out further, including writing lyrics that prominently and repeatedly featured that thing I'd said to the doorman about his dancing skills, much to the confusion of almost everyone who's heard it since. Eventually, my bandmates and I recorded a proper studio version of the song along with nine other songs and released it as a full album called *Use Your Weapons*. And thanks to no small bit of luck, "Go" was chosen as the theme song to what I consider to be easily one of the best shows on television regardless of those thirty seconds or so of familiar music they play at beginning of each episode.

I bring up my band's song "Go" not as an example of what I consider to be power pop excellence, one of those rare moments when it didn't all fall apart. In fact, if you listen to some of the YouTube comments on our video for the song, it could be argued things go immediately south as soon as my vocals come in. But it's an example of why guys and gals like me will always keep trying—you hear a melody and perhaps even a lyric to go with it in your head and you think maybe if you don't screw it up and somehow manage to find that perfect balance between frosting and cake you might just make something that would fit nicely on your record shelf alongside your favorites like Big Star, Cheap Trick, Badfinger, and—who knows—maybe even the Beatles if they were maybe only a quarter as good (which would still make them awesome). Heck, if you got really, really lucky, you could make something that you could slip into someone else's record collection without them really even noticing.

And even when that doesn't happen, it doesn't really matter anyway. Because it's in that act of trying that you suddenly realize you don't need a bunch glue and glitter to put a star on your chest after all.

It was on you this whole time.

Dave Hill *is a comedian, writer, actor, and musician. He is the author of three books,* Parking the Moose *(2019 Doubleday Canada/Penguin Random House),* Dave Hill Doesn't Live Here Anymore *(2016 Blue Rider Press), and* Tasteful Nudes *(2012 St. Martin's Press). He also plays guitar and sings in the rock bands* Valley Lodge, Painted Doll, *and* Witch Taint.

Priming the Power Pop Pump

By Ira Robbins

B OB DYLAN HAD HIS back pages; I have mine. In early 1978, in the pages of *Trouser Press*, I endeavored—with the rash hubris of know-it-all certainty—to (ite)rate the bands that comprised the power pop genre at the time. Attempts to definitively slot music into ill-defined stylistic categories are generally doomed by time, evolution, ignorance, and perspective, but attempt I did.

I was a devoted fan of power pop (or, as it was interchangeably called in those days, pop rock), and thought it opportune to use the small journalistic platform I'd helped create to promote it. Growing up in the sixties, I responded strongly to music that borrowed some of the smashed-blocked fury that made the Who my favorite band and used that rushing force to convey the AM melodies that turned me on to rock and roll in the first place. The joy of power pop for me hung suspended between musical poles, a compact confection of harmonies, velocity, ringing guitars, a solid beat, and a memorable hook, suffused with innocence and set at the fulcrum of energy and beauty, free of heavy rhythms, twelve-bar patterns, arrogance, bloat, unbridled aggression, machismo, and maturity. The strength of strings *and* the tenderness of first love.

Most of power pop's first flowering—sixties archetypes like Badfinger with the spunk of garage rock and the sweet appeal of the

Beatles—had wilted by the time arena rock was being challenged by paint-stripping punk. True, a vein of tuneful rock had run through the mid-seventies New York underground, and some of the early groups on the CBGB/Max's circuit in the direct wake of the Dolls— the Fast, Marbles, Miamis, Planets, Milk 'n' Cookies—played in and around power pop. But other than the Ramones, their ilk did not attract widespread notice and had little influence. In the rest of the world, outliers like the Nerves, Jam, Flamin' Groovies, Shoes, Motors, and others were also putting a pedal to the melody, so it didn't take much more than an educated guess to postulate, as I did in the article I wrote, that new wave (at least in the UK) and DIY (at least in the US) were about to inject power pop back into circulation. As it happened, when American labels rushed to get their piece of the end-of-the-decade youthquake, they gravitated toward the skinny-tie side of punk/new wave enthusiasm, bands with what *sounded* like commercial potential, music that wasn't mean, adversarial, political, or intimidating. In other words, colorful rocking groups with appealing tunes.

But before those clarifying events had occurred, the exponents I thought fit the bill at the beginning of 1978 were a decidedly mixed lot, not all of whom would qualify—borrowing Nick Lowe's nervously revised American album title of that year—as *Pure Pop for Now People.*

Here's the introduction that ran (in an awful script typeface) on page twenty-two of the April 1978 issue of *Trouser Press* over the headline "A Power Pop Primer":

> If one may hazard an absurd guess based on no real information, it will probably be around November of this year when some smart punk rocker will wake up and realize that a change has occurred since the inception of the new wave. In place of similar sounding four-piece

noise machines, groups that used to be called punk are replacing hoarse shouts with melody, and volume with a sense of dynamics. Not that groups have abandoned their instruments or ideals, just that a new influence has been taken on. At that point, the renaissance of power pop will have officially occurred.

Not that power pop is anything new. A few groups have always managed to hold on, even during the roughest trend, to the notion that ideal music blends songs, lyrics, and energy into a form where catchy hooks find the strength of blaring guitars a help, not a distraction. That's power pop-rock with hooks. Not tepid chart stuff like Gary Wright that uses studio musicians to lend rock credibility. Not Led Zep riff rock. Not overblown, gas-filled balloons like ELP. Not wimpy ballads like Debby Boone. Just hard rock with a beat and a melody: something you can sing on the subway or rehearse with your band. Music that'll stay with you awhile, but not too long.

Already, in fact since the beginning, there have been new wave bands devoted to power pop. Although a large segment of the bands is more blam-blam oriented, the general trend so far has been toward power pop, not away. Groups that were unheard names in the British press a year ago are turning out to be, with fair regularity, more or less pop groups that joined in the fun and got swept along by the excitement before they had a chance to explain what they were about. Generation X, Advertising, Yachts, Gorillas, and Motors are all incipient pop bands. Larger names like the Clash and Vibrators are forging strong pop-punk connections, and in America the Ramones are becoming young Beach Boys in leather jackets.

Okay, so far so good. Clearly, I wasn't making a bold prediction, just acknowledging a developing trend. So who got corralled into this club? According to me, these were the power pop acts *active* (which is why Big Star, Nazz, and the Sidewinders are AWOL; no such excuse for the absence of the Beach Boys or the Paley Brothers) at the start of 1978:

ABBA	Pezband
BTO	Piper
Bay City Rollers	Quick
Blondie	Radio Stars
Boston	Ramones
Eric Carmen	Rubinoos
Cheap Trick	Todd Rundgren
City Boy	Shoes
Clash	Slade
Dictators	Sparks
Eddie & the Hot Rods	Chris Stamey
Flamin' Groovies	Michael Stanley Band
Jam	Sweet
KISS	Dwight Twilley Band
Kursaal Flyers	Vibrators
Nick Lowe	Wings
Tom Petty	

Yeah, I know. A bit of an eye-roller, that. The assessing/predicting end of rock journalism resembles political punditry in one sense—it is *always* disheartening to see how often one has been proven wrong. But if you didn't know anything about the subsequent forty-plus years of music, maybe this blurry snapshot of 1978 doesn't seem so off base.

Today, I would keep about half of them on the list. A few had stylistic attributes that swayed me but were either dabblers

(Petty and the Hot Rods were included on the basis of a single song each) or evolvers who soon left the froth of power pop behind. Some of these acts (BTO, Slade, ABBA, KISS) fit nobody's definition of the genre. (As I declared during the interview I did a few years back for *The Power Pop Movie*, I would belatedly disqualify the Raspberries and the Knack, notwithstanding their fealty to the form's canonical audio attributes, for crimes of overt concupiscence and a dearth of winsomeness. I know that's a heretical view.)

The six-page article consisted of a few flippant sentences about each of the acts, preceded by nerdy ratings for "Pop Consciousness," "Listenability," "Disco Taint" (an absurd irrelevance, but a sign of the times, I suppose), and "Songwriting." I can't say a lot of wisdom is imparted in the piece. My abiding conviction seems to have been that a non-wimpy, noncommercial, non-pandering version of poppiness was nirvana; everything else undermined it. As a purity test, that may have missed the point, making it seem as if power pop could only thrive in a stylistic isolation ward. It's likely that few of the bands I wrote about in 1978 would have called themselves power pop, even the ones now definitively certified as such. Without knowing where any of this was headed, I clapped on a filter of my own devising and simply declared who had managed to get through it.

I called Billy Squier's *Piper* "the stinkbombs of power pop." Cheap Trick was "exactly how a pop rock band should sound." Eric Carmen's second solo album was "full of mush and marks the end of Eric the pop singer." The Clash, while "hardly a pop rock band, [had] strong pop sensibilities." The Dictators were a "pop band with big amplifiers." Boston took "the two components of power pop...and grease[d] them up to make a slick product with more hit potential than Muhammad Ali's fist." Sparks was an "irrefutable force of twinky pop and rampaging electric guitar chords." Blondie were proof that "New York punks could be a latent pop team." The Vibrators were "thought of as a British Ramones." Hey, I was younger then.

But there's an intriguing notion buried in this hindsight. Countering the usual route of a musical movement becoming diluted and dispersed over time, power pop's early days—in which a small handful of artists attempted to simultaneously mine a beloved legacy *and* pull away from simple tribute to it— were ill-defined and only came into focus with an explosion of bands who followed them. Within a few years, had there been dedicated Power Pop sections in Sam Goody and Tower stores, they would have been bursting with tremendous albums by Marshall Crenshaw, Smithereens, Elvis Brothers, Buzzcocks, Let's Active, Plimsouls, Pezband, Paul Collins' Beat, the Chords, Bram Tchaikovsky, Records, 20/20, Real Kids, Romantics, dB's, REM, Undertones, Great Buildings, Hoodoo Gurus, Tommy Keene, and many others. And they ushered in a glorious indie flood, with entire bedroom labels devoted to the sound. Velvet Crush, Adam Schmitt, the Three O'Clock, the Sneetches, the Spongetones, the Windbreakers...

Is there a lesson to be learned from this? Snapshots can capture a moment in time, but they can mislead as much as inform. While retaining its essence, power pop has traveled a great way since those naïve appraisals of 1978. I certainly could not have guessed how durable and diverse power pop would become, yielding everything from strict Beatles descendants to roaring shoegazers to twee minimalists, all finding ways to tweak the formula and still set those same old synapses snapping. The sound of innocence, at least in this corner of the musical universe, is eternal.

Ira Robbins *cofounded* Trouser Press *magazine in 1974 and was the pop music editor of* Newsday *in the nineties. In addition to five decades of music journalism, he is the author of two novels:* Kick It Till It Breaks *(2009) and* Marc Bolan Killed in Crash *(2020). He currently edits www.TrouserPress.com and is preparing an anthology/memoir.*

The Cultivation of the Cult-Pop Fan

By Mary E. Donnelly

"Bliss it was in that dawn to be alive, But to be young was very heaven."

—William Wordsworth, *The Prelude*

I WAS BORN TO be a Shoes fan. Right time, right place, right foundation.

I grew up the younger sibling of four brothers and a sister. They were, almost to a person, music obsessives.

One older brother was consumed by the Beatles. He made a tape of fifteen seconds of every Beatles song then available, in alphabetical order. He took me to *Beatlemania* for my eleventh birthday. By the time I was ten, I knew every word to every song on their US releases.

My sister, with whom I shared a room, started every day with an album. Usually the same album for months at a time. I clocked my life by her phases. Events were catalogued like a medieval archive. "In the Year of Bob Welch's *French Kiss*." "The Long Winter of Steve Miller." "The Summer of Styx."

Another brother dragged me along to the most terrifying used record store in the world. Under its low, dark ceilings—and the eye of the chain-smoking owner who looked like he kept an axe under the counter—we scrounged through bins of absolute crap, looking for the one gem that would make it all worthwhile.

He had, he says, a collection of about 5,000 singles at his peak. And we wallpapered the basement, where we younger siblings were allowed to go part feral, with full-page ads from *Billboard* and *Rolling Stone* and *Crawdaddy* standing in for *real* posters.

I learned, in junior high, that if I scraped lunch trays in the cafeteria, I got a free lunch. My mom, rewarding my effort, continued to give me forty cents a day. That was two singles a week! More than worth the social ostracism of that Darwinian system.

And so it was that I was primed to be a music obsessive, raised with such behavior normalized and even encouraged.

But I was also the first generation raised in the easily dismissed shadow of the Baby Boom: whatever we did in the dark, tumultuous fallen days of the late seventies was never as good as—could *never* be as good as—the original British Invasion and its various branches. And that pantheon was as fixed as any literary canon: the Beatles, the Stones, the Kinks. The Beach Boys and the Byrds representing proudly for the USA (but, you know, also not quite the same). And so my music obsession tended to be with those older bands, especially those that had given up the ghost by the mid-seventies, whose catalogues were conveniently complete. I liked new stuff—Elvis Costello, the Knack, the Undertones—but I knew mine was a fallen taste in a fallen world. I accepted this state of affairs as I accepted most things in my life: outwardly docile, but with an underlying restlessness.

My conversion can be traced to one night, which can be pinpointed to within a few-week window in the fall of 1979. Let's say the first or second Saturday of October. My eldest brother Paul—the Beatle brother—had an apartment the next town over, and if we younger siblings were very, very good, he'd let one of us spend a night on his couch pretty regularly. The place was a dump: a third-floor garret, ceilings not seven feet high, roof pitching lower everywhere. But the invitation was a treat: Paul had cable TV, and a great stereo, and hundreds of record albums. We could stay up late to watch *Saturday Night Live* as long as we got up for church the next day.

One day, shortly before my thirteenth birthday, Paul told me he wanted to play me something he thought I would like, so I sprawled on the sketchy carpet, ready to listen. First, he played me the Beatles' "The Night Before," a song I knew well. Then he changed the record. As the first chunky chords of "Tomorrow Night" washed over me, I sat up, like a pointer who sees movement in the bushes. He said, "I think they sound like the Beatles." I replied, "Of course they do. It's a cover." "It's *not*," he said, handing me the sleeve.

Sit with me here, on the floor. Share with me this moment of flowering, of discovery.

I was *slain*. Something was there, something for me. Not my siblings, *me*. It was…perfect. Hard and soft and crunchy and melodic, all at the same time. It's not news that "Tomorrow Night" is pretty much a platonic ideal of a pop song, but it also encapsulated the ache of adolescence, the Big Event always just out of reach. It was written for *me*. (Years later, and I wrote the book, and I know where and when it was written and why, but screw that. It was *mine*.)

Even at twelve, I was already a seasoned cynic: I had spent much of the previous summer with the previous "next Beatles," the Knack. I knew that there was likely to be a "Siamese Twins (the Monkey and Me)" hanging out there somewhere to jar me out of my pop bliss. So when "Tomorrow Night" gave way to "Too Late," I breathed a sigh of relief. And for every song after that.

"Hey, this is someone else singing," I noted, not entirely pleased with this development. "Yeah, they all sing," my brother replied, "check the inner sleeve." So I did, reluctantly tearing myself away from that weird, somewhat unsettling cover.

I'm staring at that record as I write: it's damaged. Did some basement time, did some time within reach of a claw-sharpening cat, did much time on the floor of my adolescent bedroom. There's scotch tape on the inner sleeve, and a small rip on John Murphy's cheek.

On that first night, I studied that inner sleeve with all the analytical concentration my young brain could muster, classifying and organizing the flavors and styles of the three singers and songwriters: Gary Klebe's soft-pedaled, muscular sneer; Jeff Murphy's throaty, romantic longing; John Murphy's breathy, barely concealed aggro. It was all backed by Gary and Jeff on those bipolar guitars—alternately meaty ("I Don't Miss You") and filigreed ("Every Girl")—and the solid bedrock of John's bass and Skip Meyers' drums.

There on that floor, I made uneasy truce with the strange, painful world of *Present Tense*. Because it is, almost to a song, a litany of disappointment and heartache. You would think, with all those older siblings, I would have known what a crappy breakup looked and felt like. Nope. (We were Irish: feelings were for other people.) You would think, with my thoroughgoing knowledge of Beatles lyrics, I would have parsed out the pain of love. Nope. It was there, that night, that I realized that this world of distant temptresses and petty medusas was a whole new way of looking at things. "I Don't Miss You"? "I Don't Wanna Hear It"? "Cruel You"? Whoa! Heady, dangerous stuff for a relative innocent. And I was a kid, a girl, and it had a huge impact on me. (I would later come to recognize this as the "Run for Your Life" conundrum, but that's a whole other essay.)

I listened to that album three times through that night, until Paul kicked me off his stereo and off to my couch, where it kept playing straight through my dreams. My brother's experiment had created a monster. I knew—from the first second—that I had found my band.

And here's the thing, the experience common to nearly all Shoes fans, and one of the things that sets them apart from other fandoms. For almost all of us, we were the only person like us we knew. Even my brother, who had given me my first dose, didn't fall down this rabbit hole with me. I was on my own.

That fall of 1979 was a pretty good time to be a Shoes fan. Knowing what I know now, I can see that the flurry of reviews and interviews I lovingly catalogued, and which I assumed to be the norm, was a tiny promotion blip in their career. But for me, it confirmed my view that this was a really exciting development in music; everyone seemed to be on board. I even found the PVC pressing of *Black Vinyl Shoes* in our local mall! Clearly this band was huge! I wrote a fan letter and joined the fan club—the only time in my life I have ever done such a thing.

Hey, I was twelve and turned thirteen in the middle of all this. I didn't know that the industry was cratering. I didn't know that Shoes would be handicapped as a studio band: I wouldn't have been allowed to go to concerts even if they had come to town. I had no idea how any of the business end worked. As that flurry of press fell into silence, I retired to my room with my precious clippings and vinyl and withdrew into being the only Shoes fan I knew.

I think that's why, for so many of us, Shoes feel like a personal possession. And we are possessive, even as we look for our others out there. For years, I would wear Shoes T-shirts to concerts for other bands, just to see who would react. (John Wurster, thank you for that double take at Maxwell's. You got it.) Even now, I listen to them alone, mostly. Not because I'm ashamed, or because I think others would not like them—just because they are so deeply intertwined with the lost heaven of my youth, and so, so personal.

Mary E. Donnelly *is a college professor and the coauthor of* Boys Don't Lie: A History of Shoes *(Pure Pop Press, 2013). She lives in a mountain retreat in upstate New York.*

Pop & Power:
Archie Meets Ramones

By Alex Segura

W HAT DO FOUR GRIZZLED, Queens, New York, punks with long, greasy hair and scowls that'd make a Bond villain blush have in common with five clean-cut kids from an imaginary town that might seem, at first, more Pleasantville than *Rock 'n' Roll High School*?

Quite a lot, actually, as I learned firsthand.

My day job is copresident of Archie Comics. It's a fancy title that really means I do a lot of different things—PR, editing, new business, and sometimes writing. I grew up on comics, and my introduction to the medium was *Archie*. I clearly remember my mom picking up a *Betty & Veronica Double Digest* (#14, if you must know) to keep me quiet while we waited in line at the grocery store. I was instantly hooked—pulled in by the candy colors and simple, lively line art by greats like Dan DeCarlo and Harry Lucey. I wanted to live in this magical town, and hang with these cool, clean-cut kids who knew how to have a laugh and seemed to be great friends.

Riverdale was an idyllic place, at least to a Cuban-American kid in Miami. No one's parents were divorced. There were seasons. People sang Christmas carols. But the coolest thing? They were all in a band.

The Archies as a musical entity are more Monkees than Beatles, a plot element to *The Archie Show* cartoon that became a real band, made up of session musicians and led by vocalists Ron Dante and Toni Wine. In the animated series, the group was a proto-garage band made up of the core Archie Comics characters—Archie, Jughead, Betty, Veronica, and Reggie. The kicker? The songs were great, pure pop adventure, from the powerhouse bubblegum hit "Sugar, Sugar"—with its cascading chorus and unforgettable horn riff—to its quirky, equally memorable follow-up, "Jingle Jangle." The Archies sound—crafted in the studio by (fittingly) the Monkees musical mastermind, Don Kirshner (i.e., "The Man with the Golden Ear)—was polished and funky, sugary sweet in execution with not a smidge of grit or grime. This was fun music for fun times, man.

As these things sometimes go, the animated version of the comic book characters started to influence the comics themselves, and Archie and his rock band cohorts began appearing in the pages of the *Archie* comic books. As a reader, I could never really tell what their deal was. Sometimes they seemed like down-on-their-luck nobodies struggling for attention. Other moments showed them as touring rock stars with adoring fans around the nation. (I never once thought I'd be a defining voice in their narrative over the last decade.) Either way, the Archies were cool—three fun-loving dudes, two beautiful girls, and the great, unifying force of rock music. And that damn, catchy single, "Sugar, Sugar."

◆◆◆

"COULD WE DO A Ramones comic, like you guys did with KISS?"

That was the question my buddy Matthew Rosenberg (then a rising-star comic book writer, now a big-deal comic book writer) asked me over email. He had a connection to the Ramones as they exist today, a collection of estate representatives caring for the legacy of a band with no living members. That's not a slag on them since it's actually fairly common in situations where bands become brands and founding members pass on. The fans exist, and the fans need to be sated through curation of unreleased material, reunions (where possible), and merch. We'd done a storyline in the main series, *Archie Meets KISS*, that featured Archie and his friends teaming up with Gene Simmons and his KISS crew. It was fantastical, with nods to zombie films, high school comedies, and plenty of Easter eggs. I thought that'd be it, but the Ramones? There was something.

The Ramones are as punk as punk can be, but also much more. They worshipped at the altar of "play it fast, play it hard," but the one thing that made them stand out from the pack of bands that followed them is their love for melody, and their admiration for not only the power of sixties pop bands like the Beatles, but girl groups like the Phil Spector-produced Ronettes and Shangri-Las. Spector, as many Ramones fans know, would even produce the band's 1980 album, *End of the Century*.

My point is, the Ramones could rock hard and in a way that spit in the face of bloated, seventies-era prog rock excess. Their songs pulled you in fast, with fearful tales of going down to the basement, pleas for sedation, and longing odes to potential girlfriends. To lump the Ramones in with more abrasive punk acts (which really came into being after the Ramones kicked the door down) would be foolhardy and wrong. Their musicianship was rudimentary, a trait often masked by the speed with which they strummed or banged on their instruments, but the band still knew how to craft a chorus and evoke a melody. Listening to songs like "Judy is a Punk" or "I Wanna Be Your Boyfriend" today, it's hard not to be reminded of poppier acts like the Beach Boys.

But I confess that this realization came to me late, while "researching" the story that would become *Archie Meets Ramones*. The comic is a time travel tale featuring an Archies lineup on the brink of a breakup, only to be saved by sage advice from the CBGB-era Ramones. As I dove into their musical history, I was forced to reconsider a band I had admittedly kind of written off. It's fun to be wrong sometimes.

What I (re)discovered was a group of street corner poets with New York verve and romantic hearts. Scowling punks who were able to build a garage band sound injected lovingly with a new twist—heartfelt lyrics, melodious riffs, and a leather-jacket swagger that hadn't been seen since the Beatles left Hamburg. I felt silly for writing them off, but I also felt awakened to the reality that the Ramones and the Archies weren't polar opposites, but musical cousins.

But are they power pop? As I define it, certainly. For my money, power pop is pretty literal—it's pop with oomph, whether it's the churning guitar of the Ramones' "Surfin' Bird" cover, or the funk-soaked rhythms of the Archies' ode to teen gatherings in "Archie's Party." Both bands knew when to turn up the backbeat and give their respective tunes some crunch.

Power pop covers a wide spectrum, and the Ramones and Archies represent, arguably, the endpoints—the comic book teens dancing near the edge of saccharine excess while the Queens foursome stepped on the line that borders more hardcore, less melodious punk (an area they explored later in their career, to middling success). Everything else in between? That's the wide expanse of power pop, from the lush harmonies and bombastic guitars of Elvis Costello's (and, to a degree, Paul McCartney's) "Veronica" to the grunge-tinged, retro pastiche of Weezer's "Buddy Holly," from Big Star's sludgy, pleading guitar on "September

Gurls" to the urgent jangle of Cheap Trick's "Surrender" and the sweetly sad Fountains of Wayne ballad "Hey Julie," power pop covers a lot of fertile ground.

That's the fun of it. Power pop, at its core, is about embracing joyful melody and harmonies while not being afraid to step on your reverb pedal or slam the bass drum. It's a rock song you can hum, or a pop tune with a bit of bite. That's pretty much the combined Ramones and Archies catalogues in a sentence.

The Archies might have been fabricated in a recording studio lab, but the Ramones were equally calculating in their birth, with the fake names, nods to sixties music, and a vibe that evoked fifties biker gangs. But what mattered most was the music, and the Archies and the Ramones overlapped more than I thought possible, unified by sugary choruses, melodic lyrics, and a longing for a simpler, sweeter time. In the process of creating something like *Archie Meets Ramones*, I discovered a simple truth—the bands already met long ago, and I got to discover it for myself a little later than most.

Alex Segura *is an award-winning and acclaimed writer of novels, comic books, and podcasts. He is the author of* Star Wars Poe Dameron: Free Fall, *the Pete Fernandez Mystery series (including the Anthony Award-nominated crime novels* Dangerous Ends, Blackout, *and* Miami Midnight*), and the upcoming* Secret Identity *(Flatiron Books). He has also written a number of comic books, most notably the superhero noir* The Black Ghost, *the YA music series* The Archies, *and the "Archie Meets" collection of crossovers, featuring real-life cameos from the Ramones, B-52s, and more. He is also the cocreator/cowriter of the* Lethal Lit *crime/YA podcast from iHeartRadio, which was named one of the best podcasts of 2018 by* The New York Times. *By day he is copresident of Archie Comics. A Miami native, he lives in New York with his wife and children.*

The Records

By Will Birch

FIRSTLY, I MUST THANK MY friend Paul Bradshaw for alerting me, via his mixtapes all those years ago, to some fairly obscure power pop records that came out in the wake of Big Star, Raspberries, and Badfinger (to name but three giants of the genre).

I've never much cared for the term "power pop," but I guess every movement needs a handle to aid communication. By the way, in 1994 I wrote a piece for *Mojo Magazine* in which I compiled and reviewed a C90 power pop compilation. The intro stated, "Modesty forbids me from including a track by the Records, but not from giving my former group a plug."

And the Records is what I'm remembering here, some forty years after we last toured.

In 1975 I was the drummer in a group called the Kursaal Flyers, which started life as a country rock outfit with pop tendencies. We would delight in performing the Monkees' "I'm A Believer" at our early pub gigs because jaws would drop; such was the song's potential to provoke in that hard rock era. We loved the song, of course, and by the time we had our own hit record—"Little Does She Know" (1976, CBS)—we were fast moving in the pop direction. Then we disbanded and my thoughts turned to forming a new group that would attempt to emulate the sounds the Beatles and the Byrds circa 1966.

In 1977 John Wicks had joined the Kursaals, on rhythm guitar, and he cowrote with our singer Paul Shuttleworth a song called "Moral Fibre." It sounded like the Move, and I immediately recognized in John a tunesmith who might bring my own lyrics to life. We had a chat and in the spring of 1978 John and I quickly wrote a batch of songs, including "Teenarama" and "Up All Night." Then we advertised in the *Melody Maker* for a bass player and a guitarist. We envisaged a classic four-piece of uniform height and head-to-body ratio.

Phil Brown turned up toting a Rickenbacker bass and considerable charisma and was immediately recruited. Finding a lead guitarist was not so easy; a chap named Brian Alterman joined us and we recorded some demos courtesy of CBS to whom I was still signed, but Brian suddenly quit. Among the many guitarists we subsequently auditioned was one Huw Gower. As soon as Huw plugged in his leftie Gibson 335 and demonstrated some simulated backward guitar, we knew he was the guy. We had a chat about Moby Grape and Spirit (with whom Huw was familiar) and rehearsals ensued.

Although we were far from ready, I pushed for live gigs in order to establish the Records, a name I had dreamt up in the bath. I thought that if we didn't get the name out there fast, someone else might claim it, a bit like securing a domain name today. We played the pubs and clubs, somehow appeared on London Weekend TV, went on tour opening for Wilko Johnson, and recorded more demos. CBS expressed interest, but in the midst of the discussions our then-manager went off on a French vacation. We were affronted by this and resolved to fire him, which led to a series of events that would inspire the song "Starry

Eyes." Ultimately CBS passed and we found a new manager and he started hawking our demos around.

It was during the summer of 1978 that we received a call from Stiff Records asking if we would like to join that autumn's Be Stiff Tour as backing group to Rachel Sweet. Rachel had recorded a song John and I had written entitled "Pin a Medal on Mary," so that was the connection. We rather cheekily asked Stiff for our own spot in the show and amazingly they agreed. We were now on the train—the tour traveled the UK for six weeks by British Rail.

The Stiff tour had the honor of kicking off the fastest-moving twelve months of our lives, which were dramatically accelerated when the show was booked to play four nights at New York's Bottom Line. For most of us in the thirty-strong touring party it was to be our first visit to the USA. By now the Records had recorded "Starry Eyes" and released it on 45. We were also about to sign with Virgin Records. I recall a pre-signing meeting at which Richard Branson told us that "to make the deal viable," Virgin needed to secure the publishing rights to our original songs. As I rose from my chair, ready to walk out, Branson uttered, "Oh come, come," and we settled on an arrangement whereby the original songs' copyrights would revert to the writers after ten years.

In early 1979, with "Starry Eyes" getting US airplay, we started recording our debut LP, *Shades in Bed*, with producer Robert John "Mutt" Lange and engineer Tim Friese-Greene. Songs included "Teenarama," "Affection Rejected," "All Messed Up and Ready to Go," and "Girls That Don't Exist," an old Kursaals song I cowrote with our bassist Richie Bull. We also recorded a cover of Tim Moore's "Rock and Roll Love Letter," which was regrettably omitted from the album after it bombed on 45.

In the USA, our album would be distributed by Atlantic, who represented the Virgin label there. The Americans retitled it *The Records* and revamped the sleeve, which involved Atlantic's art director and a photographer coming to London carrying an illuminated "The Records" sign. The photo session took place in the wholly unique atmosphere of Dobell's jazz record shop in London's Shaftesbury Avenue.

In May we went on a UK tour opening for the Jam. We were a few years older than Paul Weller's group and his youthful audiences didn't really take to us, but the experience was invaluable as preparation for our first full American tour. We set off that August for eight whole weeks in the land of neon. The US was an eye-opener; acts whose records I had previously collected, such as the dB's and the Rubinoos, opened for us! Conversely, we supported others, including dates with Joe Jackson and opening for the Cars in Central Park. We also appeared with the Cars on *The Midnight Special* TV show.

The Virgin/Atlantic publicity machine never slept as our debut LP scaled the charts. In every town we played there were numerous interviews, radio station visits, in-store appearances, and a more or less sold-out show. It must be a familiar story for any group "breaking" America. Your record promotion guy accompanies you to the key radio stations and you discover he's on first-name terms with all of the programmers and DJs. You ask yourself, "How come this guy has so many friends?" and perhaps in some dark office down the hallway you get a glimpse.

Songwriters that you've covered turn up at your shows, sometimes bearing tapes. In our case, Tim Moore and Blue Ash's Frank Secich (we covered "Abracadabra (Have You Seen Her?)" on our *High Heels* EP). You meet stars: in LA, the legendary Kim Fowley; on Long Island, Billy Joel, who comes backstage for a spot of tie-swapping; and Flo & Eddie show up everywhere. In

Cleveland your phone rings at eight in the morning and a female voice asks, "Which one are you in the photograph?"

Following our 1979 US tour we commenced the recording of our next LP, *Crashes*, with producer Craig Leon. We'd met Craig in Toronto where he was producing the B-Girls and we knew his name from early LPs by the Ramones and Blondie. Craig came to London and we cut some tracks at Air Studios. We also played dates in Europe, opening for Robert Palmer, but soon after this, Huw left the group. The trouble had started a few months earlier, in Detroit. It was on stage, halfway through our song "The Same Mistakes" (which Huw had introduced, veering wildly off-script) that John and I looked at each other across the stage, sharing the same inevitable thought. Back in London, Huw was summoned to a group meeting. He was the last to arrive, and he walked in and said, "Don't tell me...I'm fired." Our manager replied, "Well, Huw, er, the Records, that is John and Will, have decided, er, they no longer require your services."

Firing Huw may have been a mistake; if you have a dissenter on board but they are part of the original magic that made it happen, no matter what it takes, maybe try and find a work-around. Maybe. But Huw was gone and in early 1980 we cut more backing tracks with Craig Leon producing and former Kursaals' guitarist Barry Martin stepping in for the sessions. We were now looking for a permanent lead guitarist and Craig suggested nineteen-year-old Jude Cole. I'd recently seen Jude, a great guitarist and singer, with Moon Martin at the Marquee. Jude flew in and instantly clicked. His soaring harmony vocals blended so well with John's and enhanced our sound, particularly on "Girl in Golden Disc." We recorded at the Townhouse, with the Jam in the adjoining studio, working on their LP *Sound Affects*. We invited Paul Weller to listen to playbacks of "Spent a Week With You

Last Night" and "I Don't Remember Your Name," both heavily influenced by the Beatles' *Revolver*. "I don't think you'll get away with it" were Paul's only words. Then we heard the Jam's new 45 "Start!" which sounded like the Beatles' "Taxman" backward!

A US tour was arranged to promote *Crashes* and its offspring 45, "Hearts in Her Eyes," which had also been covered beautifully by the Searchers. In direct contrast to the previous year's outing, there was scant promotion; whereas in 1979 a stretch limo met us at the airport to whisk us into Manhattan, where we were greeted outside the Gramercy Park Hotel by autograph hunters (rumored to be extras hired by our PR to help raise our spirits after a long flight), we now had to board a public bus at JFK, musical equipment in hand. Whereas in 1979 we did seven interviews a day, we were about to do hardly any interviews in seven weeks. Maybe *Crashes* was a turkey; maybe it was because our debut album had been the first release under the Virgin/Atlantic pact and *Crashes*, merely one year later, was apparently the last, but the honeymoon was over.

After the tour ended in Chicago, Jude stayed in the USA while John, Phil, and I returned home, unsure of our next move. We then fell out with our manager, largely because some of our gear had failed to make it back home. The inevitable court case followed and dragged on for months. We won, but we were now reduced to a trio with no live work and just a ragged portfolio of bitter new songs. We were on the verge of disintegration but then, amazingly, Virgin picked up its option for a third album! It put us in a state of shock, but we rehearsed, we demoed, we plotted, and we auditioned.

It was decided, perhaps unwisely, to recruit a lead singer, or "front man." His name was Chris Gent, a good guy. We also enrolled an able guitarist by the name of Dave Whelan and proceeded to make *Music on Both Sides*. I was tired of playing drums and, as the album's "producer," enrolled the great Bobby Irwin to thump the tubs on my behalf. In 1981 we went to Virgin's The Manor Studio and laid down tracks, then did overdubs and mixing at the Townhouse. But we knew in our hearts that what little magic we possessed two years earlier had now waned. A single, "Imitation Jewellery," was released, but the LP languished on Virgin's shelf for a year before it was pressed up and perfunctorily distributed, which was really all it deserved. As a quintet we played two final gigs in London in 1982 before calling it quits.

We attempted to reform the group on several occasions, the last being in 1992 when we played just one date, in Kingston upon Thames. And, as is the case with many music acts that had had a brief brush with success in the distant past, there was always the persistent, nagging thought of reforming again for one last ride. After all, we had loved touring in America where we still had a small but dedicated following, and "Starry Eyes" continued to enjoy classic status on various hit lists and compilations. There were some informal discussions, but nothing came of them probably due to geography as John now lived in America, as did Jude of course, while Phil and I were in the UK. John kept the name alive, still playing shows as "The Records" in California, and of course he had our blessing. Then, in 2012, Phil sadly died, and John died six years later. It is to those two much-missed friends and essential talents that this piece is dedicated.

Will Birch *is a former drummer and songwriter with the Kursaal Flyers and the Records. During the 1980s he moved into record production working with such acts as Any Trouble, Dr Feelgood, Billy Bremner (Rockpile) and the Long Ryders. Birch has written articles for* Mojo *and other music magazines and published three books:* No Sleep Till Canvey Island—The Great Pub Rock Revolution; Ian Dury—The Definitive Biography; *and* Cruel To Be Kind—The Life & Music of Nick Lowe.

No Substitute:
The Story of the Shivvers

By John M. Borack

D URING THE HALCYON DAYS of power pop in the late
seventies/early eighties, independently released 45s by
artists from all over the globe began springing up like so many
melodic weeds. In the United States, long-forgotten combos such
as the Names (hailing from Illinois), the Reruns (Michigan), and
the Shake Shakes (hometown unknown) released one or two such
singles and eventually faded from view, with their scant, difficult-
to-track-down recorded output left to be coveted by collectors
and power pop cultists.

Wisconsin had their own "one (or two) and done" power
pop upstarts during that era in the Shivvers. The five-piece band
produced only one single—1980's sublime and now hopelessly
rare "Teen Line" backed with "When I Was Younger"—but differed
from most of their contemporaries in that they were fronted by a
woman. Jill Kossoris not only served as the Shivvers' lead vocalist
but also penned most of their songs and added keyboards to the
mix. Perhaps most importantly, Kossoris also had the musical
vision of what the Shivvers would one day become: a powerhouse
live act performing three-minute nuggets that incorporated the
band's love of sixties music with a palpable sense of urgency.

◆◆◆

KOSSORIS GREW UP IN a family where music was always in the mix. "Music played constantly in our house," she remembers. "My dad played Beethoven and Fats Waller, mom played Sinatra, and my sister dug the Beatles and the Stones." Family strife also played a part in the Kossoris family's love of music. "My parents did not have a good marriage—there was not a lot of conversation or discussion—so a lot of that silent tension was relieved and expressed in the music they played," she says.

Like so many musicians who grew up in the sixties, Kossoris was awestruck by four young men from Liverpool. "The night of the Beatles' debut on *The Ed Sullivan Show*, I was sent to bed early," she reminisces. "Little did my family know that the forbidden aspect of not being allowed to watch only increased my interest." A four-year-old Kossoris recalls being in bed and hearing what she describes as "this unearthly sound of excitement." Unable to tolerate the curiosity any longer, she snuck down the hallway to peek around the corner and catch a glimpse of the TV. Her immediate reaction? "The sight was as exciting as the sound!"

The experience lit a spark in the young girl: "I wondered why anyone would want to do anything else. I also wondered why no girls were in the band." The next year Kossoris began taking piano lessons and joined her first band at age fourteen; that combo, dubbed Coffee and Cream as a nod to their interracial makeup, "performed Jackson 5 and Al Green songs in the basement," Kossoris says. Several other bands followed, with Kossoris gaining confidence with each step. Around 1977, she joined the unfortunately named In a Hot Coma, which included future Shivvers bassist Scott Krueger and drummer Jim Richardson. Eventually, Kossoris's desire to express herself creatively led to her and Richardson plotting a new band. Guitarists Mike Pyle and Jim Eannelli were recruited, and in 1978, the Shivvers were born. "I wanted to make people feel like I felt when I heard a great song or saw a great band," Kossoris explains.

Kossoris didn't form the band to specifically travel the then-current power pop route, but she admits, "power pop as defined by Pete Townsend and epitomized by those early Who singles was definitely an influence, but so was ABBA, Motown, girl groups, and the Stooges."

Guitarist Mike Pyle remembers, "I wanted to do pop stuff for sure, but I started to get a real education when Jill and Jim started suggesting songs. That was my favorite time...covering the Beatles, Beau Brummels, Dave Clark Five, Supremes, Flamin' Groovies, and the Honeycombs, then mixing in some pop-punk like Tuff Darts and Generation X. We really followed Jill and Jim's sensibility."

Kossoris elaborates: "When I think of the term 'pop,' I think of an extremely well-crafted song without a lot of wasted space; a compact work with no downtime, long solos, or boring bits and very direct lyrics, just like the old hit singles...like Brill Building songwriting. Motown is perfectly crafted pop with a dose of rhythm and soul. Any great song has power, [whether it's] emotionally, rhythmically, melodically, or lyrically; the truly great [tunes] contain all those elements."

At the time, the relatively novel idea of a female-fronted indie rock band presented a few challenges for Kossoris. "By the time of the Shivvers, I had learned what kind of people I wanted to work with and what kind of people I didn't," she admits. "I'd been demeaned, harassed, and ridiculed enough (even in daily life for wanting to be in a band and being a bit of an eccentric) to know that I wanted to be treated respectfully. I didn't want any special treatment, but I wanted to be treated as an equal. It was very uncommon for a young girl to be in a band in the late seventies, and frankly, most people didn't know what to make of it."

Kossoris quickly understood the double standards female-fronted groups faced back then. "The worst part about being a female in a band was being constantly judged by your looks, and sometimes solely by your looks. While I completely understand that visual image is extraordinarily important, I think charisma comes in all forms. It also makes you overly self-conscious, and self-consciousness can kill art. I am glad to see that this attitude has loosened up a bit in the last couple decades."

"Jill had very clear feelings about pretty much everything," Pyle adds. "Direction. Strong instincts. A sense of style." Kossoris agrees, saying, "I didn't want people to come see us because there was a girl dancing around in a low-cut top!" The Shivvers gigged in and around Milwaukee for several years, wowing crowds with their mix of originals and covers. Pyle fondly recalls the band's first gig, at a club called Zak's: "The dance floor was packed. I can still see people's faces, smiling and dancing…in a punk club! [We played 'Be My Baby'] and it went on and on, crescendo after crescendo. It made the hair stand up on the back of your neck." The quintet also shared stages with like-minded acts such as Shoes and the Romantics and even opened for Iggy Pop ("He's a gem," says Kossoris), as well as covering his tune "Take Care of Me" in their live set.

The band's original material was an invigorating amalgamation of their various sixties influences (girl group, garage rock, Merseybeat), with Kossoris's sassy, pleading lead vocals meshing perfectly with the band's sharp instrumental prowess. The only Shivvers recordings released during the band's life span were the power pop classic "Teen Line" (written by Kossoris about her budding romance with Scott Krueger, aided and abetted by lengthy telephone conversations) and "When I Was Younger," a bit of a banger with an instrumental intro reminiscent of the Who's "I Can See For Miles" and a girl-group-influenced bridge. The single (which today sells for between $350 and $700, if a copy can be found) garnered rave reviews from tastemaker publications such as *Bomp!* and *New York Rocker*, sending the Shivvers on the hunt for the always-elusive record deal. At this point, a power pop icon entered the picture.

◆◆◆

KOSSORIS BECAME A HUGE fan of Raspberries after hearing "Go All the Way" ("Nothing else sounded like that in 1972") and the band's other hits on AM radio. "To this day, there are very few hit songs and performances with that much energy and passion; those Raspberries singles are some of the greatest radio songs of all time," she enthuses. She even spearheaded having Raspberries perform live at her high school in 1974 by forging signatures of her classmates in order to win a contest.

Kossoris remained a fan of post-Raspberries Eric Carmen and picks up the story: "I was a member of his fan club, 'The Carmen Connection.' Through them I was able to get a VHS tape to Eric of a few songs we did on a local TV show hoping he would be interested in producing us…and he called! We spoke several times about possible record labels and discussed [the Shivvers] doing a few Raspberries songs, but I remember telling him that those songs were not just great songs, they were great performances, and I didn't know if anyone could recapture that." According to Kossoris, Carmen seemed surprised by her assessment, perhaps because Raspberries were not as highly regarded at that time (1980) as they are today.

(As an aside, the Shivvers did have a go at a few Eric Carmen tunes over the course of their career: they recorded "Get the Message," a Carmen-penned number originally released by his pre-Raspberries band Cyrus Erie, but the only mix-down of the recording was inadvertently erased. Live, the band doled out spirited versions of Carmen solo cuts "It Hurts Too Much" and "Hey Deanie.")

"The idea was for us to find a label and then we would discuss production [with Eric]," Kossoris continues. "We submitted demos to Arista and Elektra and they both passed. I told Eric and he said something like, 'Most of these people wouldn't know a cool band if they heard it—they wear socks with sandals.'"

Kossoris also recalls Bomp! Records being interested in signing the Shivvers, but sadly, no record deal ever came to pass. Looking back, Kossoris says, "We probably should have moved to California and started really courting the labels like Tom Petty did. There's no guarantee we would have been a success, but I wish we could have at least had an opportunity to reach our potential."

Pyle seconds Kossoris's thoughts. "Of course, it would have been great to be picked up by supportive management, make a record and tour to get some exposure, stay together ten years, and make a few more records. But we are talking about five people doing this one thing together but each having a very different experience, especially the last six months or so. Bands get complicated."

Said complications and a growing sense of frustration led to the Shivvers imploding and disbanding in 1982. For most bands, that would have been the end of the story. But some twenty years after the band's breakup, a Shivvers fan contacted Kossoris out of the blue, leading to the band's single—as well as their previously unissued recordings—being discovered by a new generation of power pop fans.

♦♦♦

"THAT WOULD BE CHUCK Warner at Hyped to Death Records," Kossoris says. "I had grown quite dispirited and disheartened by the time Chuck contacted us. He sent us an email after hearing 'Teen Line' asking if we had any more songs, and that he'd like to release them. I was initially very indifferent [because] it was actually kind of painful to look back on those songs, but he was so enthusiastic I thought, 'What do we have to lose?'"

Warner's enthusiasm led to the limited release of two now-rare Shivvers CD compilations in 2002 and 2006. The twenty-track 2006 disc, subtitled *Lost Hits from Milwaukee's First Family of Powerpop: 1979–1982*, contains most of the band's studio output, as well as seven smokin' live cuts dating from 1980 to 1982, and two excellent recordings from a partial Shivvers reunion in 1989. The fidelity isn't the best, but the sheer strength of the songs and the band's inherent passion shines brightly on the studio recordings and the live tracks: "Rather Be Lonely," for example, finds the band exploring their Motown influences with Kossoris coming off sounding like Chrissie Hynde singing "Cool Jerk." "Baby's Blue Eyes" showcases the band's distinct Rockpile influence and Pyle's love of rockabilly.

And that was that—until 2014, when another indie label, Sing Sing Records, picked up the mantle, cleaned up the original recordings, and released *The Shivvers*, a collection that Kossoris says would have been the band's debut LP back in the day. A dozen tracks, no filler; just song after song of youthful passion and expert melodicism. "'No Substitute' and 'Please Stand By' are probably the most representative songs of what the Shivvers actually sounded like, but 'Remember Tonight' is the song I'm most proud of because it's more musically complex, moody and harder to categorize," Kossoris says.

Pyle says he's most fond of "Why Tell Lies." "It was one of our earliest tunes and it was the first time I saw a song come together, be arranged and take shape," he says. "It gave an indication of what the band was to sound like." Pyle also cites the uber-catchy "No Substitute" as "pretty much a perfect pop song with a great arrangement." The album was issued on vinyl only and turned out to be Sing Sing's final release; as such, it quickly fell out of print.

In 2020, however—forty years after the Shivvers' lone single was originally released— St. Louis's Rerun Records and Austria's Bachelor Records released *The Shivvers* on vinyl and compact disc. "Most of our songs were recorded on two-inch analog tape, and a few of the songs were only available on cassette," Kossoris says. "The 2020 reissue sounds even better than the 2014 Sing Sing release because the ability to clean up sound on older recordings is always advancing."

The surviving members of the Shivvers are all still involved in music in various configurations. "This was not a hobby or a fad for any of us," Kossoris says. "We are all lifers!" Kossoris and Scott Krueger still write together, while Pyle plays with a Boston-area band called Hummingbird Syndicate.

When asked about the Shivvers' legacy, Pyle ponders the question, then replies, "A really good band. Authentic. We put a lot of energy and spirit into our recordings and shows. I hope it gets rediscovered over and over. It would have been great to make a big splash, but I think we left a mark."

Jill Kossoris adds, "If people are responding to the Shivvers, it could be because it's rare to hear a band that hasn't been reshaped by a record label executive, manager, agent, or producer. We never sold out; we ran purely on instinct, inspiration, and the love of rock 'n' roll, and I think you can hear that."

John M. Borack *is a veteran music journalist who currently serves as a contributing editor at* Goldmine Magazine, *a monthly music collectors' periodical. Borack is also the author of three books: 2008's* Shake Some Action: The Ultimate Power Pop Guide, *2010's* John Lennon: Life Is What Happens, *and 2018's* Shake Some Action 2.0: A Guide to the 200 Greatest Power Pop Albums 1970-2017. *His next book,* The Beatles 100, *is scheduled for publication via Rare Bird in 2021. He lives in Orange County, California, and is exceedingly proud of his children and his ever-expanding music and memorabilia collection.*

Teenage News
(An Ode to Greg Shaw)

By Patrick DiPuccio

*"The first time I ever heard about Greg Shaw was from the owner of
Aquarius Records in North Beach, San Francisco, circa 1974. 'There's
a guy in LA, Greg Shaw, he has a label called Bomp! You should get in
touch with him.' Greg brought power pop to America."*

—Paul Collins, The Nerves/The Beat

"Invite me to your wedding."

IT ISN'T EVERY DAY that one of your musical influences makes
that kind of request. But Greg Shaw did after I told him I met
my wife-to-be in the produce section of the Toluca Lake Trader
Joe's. She sported a Bomp! Records T-shirt, and if she'd been
wearing anything else we may never have talked. That's just one
of the many strange and wonderful ways I crossed paths with
the former editor of *Phonograph Record* magazine and founder
of *Who Put the Bomp* magazine (later changed to simply *Bomp!*)
and Bomp! Records. I hadn't really put it all together until I sat
down to write this essay.

"I like your fanzine…"

ONE HOT SUMMER DAY, lounging around a pool in Whittier,
California, some of my high school friends and I decided to

start a fanzine. We called it *Flipside*, with a dual mindset of promoting an alternative Los Angeles Eastside journalistic point of view as well as referencing the sometimes-overlooked B-sides of singles. The year was 1977, and the punk/new wave scene was beginning to erupt in LA. We had very little knowledge about magazine publishing, but with fanzines from the UK and publications from the US to guide us, we pulled together our first issue. *Who Put the Bomp!* magazine had an unquestionable influence on *Flipside*. We enjoyed both the graphics and the corresponding content. Each issue showcased its own musical viewpoint. For instance, the psychedelic colors of the historic power pop issue exploded from the record store shelves, capturing perfectly the energy contained in that issue's featured theme.

Bomp! magazine was chock full of insightful articles, reviews, and pictures by some of the very best writers and photographers at the time, familiar names like Metal Mike Saunders, Lester Bangs, John Mendelssohn, and Anastasia Pantsios. When we finally met Greg and he mentioned liking our 'zine, we took it as a compliment of the highest order. For kids like us to not only meet him but to also be accepted into his community made us feel pretty special.

I was familiar with Greg from his writing in *Creem* magazine, but started to pay more attention to him during his *Phonograph Record* magazine days. I'd rush down to the nearest record store every week to grab a copy, bring it home, and immediately absorb every page. With Greg often at the helm, many of the reviews, ads, and stories highlighted artists like Roy Wood, ABBA, Dr. Feelgood, and Badfinger. He made sure the criticism never got too pedantic, and that the issue was an enjoyable read. For example, there was a wonderful column called "Blind Date" penned by Flo and Eddie (Howard Kaylan and Mark Volman of the Turtles). Coeditor Ken Barnes would assign the duo records to listen to without their knowing who the artists were. They'd comment about the song, the performance, or any other thing that came into their heads. It was a way to involve the reader in a quasi-personal experience.

The approach was fresh, lively, and humorous, inspiring the way *Flipside* reviewed discs in our early issues. When it came time to do record reviews, our little staff would congregate at one of our houses, put on a record (B-side first, naturally), then make comments about it. We might chat about the music, lyrics, record sleeve, or whatever else would come to mind. After recording what we said onto a cassette, we would transcribe the comments, then print them verbatim in our fanzine.

Another *Phonograph Record* magazine columnist when Greg was the editor was the legendary Rodney Bingenheimer. His man-on-the-scene approach made you feel like you were in the clubs right alongside him. Because we enjoyed his obvious passion for "happening" music as evidenced by his writing and his KROQ radio show, we wanted Rodney to be a part of our 'zine. Rodney graced *Flipside* with his radio show's top twenty song listings for two decades, an honor we never took lightly.

Now, I knew nothing of Greg's first foray into self-publishing, but discovering *Bomp!* made me realize I was not the only guy into the types of music featured in its pages. There was a whole world out there for geeks like me who were into garage band power pop. It turned out there were others around with an affinity for groups like Artful Dodger, the Sweet, and Raspberries. When it came to power pop, Greg Shaw was a legend, supporting and turning folks on to artists we loved, didn't know, or should've been paying more attention to.

"Greg loved music and built a business from his passion. Bomp! released 20/20's first single and some other tracks through the years. He shined his light on a lot of music and helped spread the word. We're forever grateful for everything he did for us."

—Steve Allen (20/20)

The vitality of the LA power pop scene from the late seventies into the eighties burst out from the local stages of the Starwood, Whisky, Troubadour, both Madame Wong's and Wong's West, Music Machine, Club 88, Hong Kong Café, and other venues. On any given night, one could see a number of bands under the "new wave" banner, several referencing the 1960s British Invasion in their fashion and musical approach. In the post-Knack signing boom, the Pop, 20/20, the Beat, Candy, and other musically minded outfits garnered major label deals. With his blond Keith Relf hair, and often wearing a turtleneck sweater, Greg could be seen standing in the crowd at a concert surveying everything around him, watching the interaction of the audience with the entertainers on stage. He exuded a sort of contentment, being completely at home in his rock and roll environment. Smiling and relaxed, Greg was always open to a quick hello or assessment of the evening's events and goings on within the Bomp! community.

He was very supportive of the local and national music scenes, and with the help of his partner Suzy, released seminal singles by LA acts like the Last, the Zeros, the Nerves, and the Pandoras, and included artists like Tommy Rock, Kim Fowley, and Paul Collins on compilations. With his assistance, singles like "Johnny Are You Queer?" by Josie Cotton, Devo's version of "Satisfaction," and the Plimsouls' "A Million Miles Away" shepherded those performers to major label contracts. Greg also put out albums and singles by acts from outside of LA like Stiv Bators, Iggy Pop, Flamin' Groovies, the Modern Lovers, the Steppes, the Choir, and the Romantics. Of course, I'd be lax if I didn't mention his championing of LA's Paisley Underground scene.

We used to drive from the San Gabriel Valley to the diminutive Bomp! record store on Laurel Canyon Boulevard to either restock *Flipside* or just hang out during signings by the likes of Blondie, the Damned, and Dead Boys. Any Bomp! in-store appearance was an occasion not to be missed. Local scenesters would mingle with the advertised band and cavort on the street outside or in the back alley. That was one of the only spots in the LA region you could get up-to-date import singles, hard-to-find releases, and the newest issues of fanzines and periodicals from other countries.

Whenever I'd take a trip out of town, Greg would be my guide to the hot spots and regional talent in the city I was visiting. His tourist guide to the San Francisco Bay Area in *Phonograph Record* magazine turned me on to the fantastic Rather Ripped record shop in Berkeley. In addition to being an excellent local establishment, right off the University of California campus, it had the distinction of being the home of Beserkley ("Home of the Hits") Records. I stopped into the place, and was surprised the man behind the counter turned out to be Gary Phillips, one of the guitarists of the band Earthquake. We chatted a bit, and I ended up purchasing the fantastic *Beserkley Chartbusters Volume 1* album (with the Rubinoos, Greg Kihn, Jonathan Richman, and others) and Earthquake's *Rockin' the World* disc (still in my top five all-time live albums). Before I headed out to visit my folks in North Carolina in 1978, Greg suggested I check out the Chapel Hill pop outfit Sneakers, featuring pre-dB's Chris Stamey, Will Rigby, and soon to be famed producer Mitch Easter.

"I'm working on this concept I'm thinking of calling Bubble Punk."

GREG GAVE ME A demo someone had sent him where the hook was simply "Oh, wow. Oh, wow." He thought by fusing a light bubblegum song with a fast and heavy attack, he would create a new musical form. He enjoyed combining different types of music together to create original genres. So, off I went back to my hometown of Whittier to lay down a demo on a friend's tape recorder. When I returned to Bomp! headquarters and played it for Greg, he felt I'd made it more complex than what he was looking for. That ended my involvement with that short-lived project. Fortunately, the group Blow-Up was meeting with Greg at the time and loved the Big Muff fuzz pedal sound I used on the demo. They were previewing an unreleased New York Dolls song they'd recorded for a possible Bomp! single that ultimately never came out ("Teenage News" backed with "Hanging Out At The 7-Eleven"). When they asked me to join their combo as a guitarist, the possibility of playing behind a potential single on Bomp! enticed me to climb aboard.

"You know Phil from Phil and the Frantics?"

THAT WOULD HAVE BEEN Phil Kelsey (aka Devin Payne), who produced Blow-Up's demos at Pasha Studios for CBS. During the sessions, Devin said he'd fronted a band in Phoenix produced by Waylon Jennings in the 1960s (the aforementioned Frantics).

I would drop into Greg's office occasionally to say "hello," and when I told him I knew Phil he became very excited. He was well aware of the ensemble, and wanted to talk with Devin about possibly releasing some of the Frantics recordings. After I'd introduced them to each other, they combined to release an album, which came out as part of the *Rough Diamonds: History of*

Garage Band Music series (the single "I Must Run" had previously appeared on *Pebbles Volume 2*). That album has since been rereleased on other labels, but not surprisingly it was Bomp! that took the initiative to reintroduce the pop world to Phil and the Frantics.

> "Greg Shaw was a quiet, thoughtful, and clever guy...once you really knew him he relaxed...laughed, and you could really talk about anything...we chatted about the books he was reading...the books I had recently read...and music, of course...though he was a lowkey guy...he really did brighten up any room that he snuck into."

—John Fallon (the Steppes)

Greg's death in 2004 took us all by surprise. There'd be no more spending time at his record-filled office, or running into him at a show. *Flipside* had ceased publication officially in early 2002, so I hadn't stayed in contact with him on a regular basis. Not having Greg around left a noticeable hole in the community. The disappearance of his positivity and vision of what made something groovy led to an unraveling of the cultural fabric that unified many of us. Bomp! had been an inspirational compass, and the focus of the scene became less clear and more fragmented in the ensuing years. Every now and then I'd run into Suzy at the local post office, and it felt nice to still have that connection to him present in my life.

Only a few weeks after Greg passed away, I married Ann, my Trader Joe's lady with the Bomp! shirt. Our nuptials took place at a small Catholic church up the street from Al's Bar, a notorious punk rock club where the *Flipside* crew often held court. I made sure to thank Greg in my wedding reception speech, followed by a short set of songs with a few of my ex-Blow-Up (and then-current Condors) bandmates. It would've been nice to have him there, but his spirit was certainly felt by us.

"I thought about you when the radio played"
—The Plimsouls "A Million Miles Away"

NOWADAYS, I MIGHT BE DRIVING down the road when a really cool tune comes on a station. That's when Greg will pop into my mind, making me smile and causing me to accelerate just a little bit more.

PATRICK DIPUCCIO

Patrick DiPuccio *(a.k.a. Pooch) was the cofounding editor of* Flipside *fanzine. He fronts the band the Condors and was a member of a number of groups over the years including Blow-Up and the Sloths.*

Pat would also like to give a sincere thanks to Ann Kiuchi and Harvey Kubernik for their continued help and support.

Yellow Pills
(And Other Gateway Drugs)

By S. W. Lauden

GREAT POWER POP SONGS are addictive. The best ones deliver a consistent dose of sugary hooks and sweet melodies served up with a jolt of infectious energy. We score them at record stores, on internet radio shows and algorithmic playlists. Or maybe you hear one between bands at a club, edging over to discreetly ask the DJ where you can get some more. These are the songs we use to turn others onto the genre we love.

But most great power pop songs aren't over-the-counter fixes. They can't be measured by chart positions or endless spins on classic rock radio. These songs stay in circulation thanks to the dedication and devotion of die-hard fans (and occasional film and TV placements). I'm not talking about anomalous commercial successes like "Go All The Way" by Raspberries or "My Sharona" by the Knack; I mean the street-grade "should've been smash hits" like "September Gurls" by Big Star, "Too Late" by Shoes, "Teen Line" by the Shivvers, "Girl Of My Dreams" by Bram Tchaikovsky, or "Sparky's Dream" by Teenage Fanclub. It's undeniable that certain songs have become gateway drugs to power pop.

"Yellow Pills" by 20/20 is one of those songs. A perennial power pop classic from the band's self-titled 1979 debut album on Portrait

Records, "Yellow Pills" was originally the B-side to the first single "Tell Me Why (Can't Understand You)" (itself a shining example of the genre at its peak). There's no doubt that *20/20* is one of the most revered power pop albums of all time, but it has deeper meanings and more personal connections for many longtime fans. "It's not only a wonderful rock and roll record, it was a game changer for me. I think it's pretty safe to say that had I not heard this album back in 1980, I may not have become a music journalist, and author, who writes quite a bit about power pop," said John M. Borack, who named *20/20* number one in *Shake Some Action 2.0: A Guide to the 200 Greatest Power Pop Albums*.

Other excellent tracks on *20/20* include the pleading love song "Cheri"; the Bowie-meets-sixties garage stomp of "Out of This Time"; the dreamy, latter-day glam of "Jet Lag"; and the upbeat urgency of "Remember the Lightning." All fantastic songs, but it was "Yellow Pills" that went on to have a life of its own after the band first broke up in 1983. This is largely thanks to a slew of reverent compilations—like *Poptopia!: Power Pop Classics Of The '70s* (Rhino Records)—and Jordan Oakes' legendary nineties namesake fanzine and seminal power pop collections. All further proof that dedicated fans will never let a truly great power pop song fade into obscurity.

"I bought and immediately fell in love with the first 20/20 album in 1980. About ten years later, when trying to think of a good name for my fanzine, 'Yellow Pills' came to mind. It seemed to fit," Oakes said. "It was meant to pay tribute to a quintessential power pop band."

Just what makes "Yellow Pills" so timeless, though, is a matter for debate (lord knows power poppers love a good debate). Is it the syrupy, too-cool-for-school drug culture vocals (with an oblique nod to "Mother's Little Helper" by the Rolling Stones)?

The hyper-stylized music and relentless, four-on-the-floor mid-tempo groove? The undeniably hooky, soaring chorus that erupts from the verses like some kind of Beatles-y phoenix? Whatever your personal opinions, there's something about "Yellow Pills"—and all the best power pop songs—that is far greater than the sum of its parts.

On top of it all, "Yellow Pills" is a quintessential LA power pop anthem. Which is why it's so incredible that the song's origin story starts in Tulsa, Oklahoma. That's where 20/20 guitarist Steve Allen first met his future songwriting partner and lifelong friend, Ron Flynt, the summer before sixth grade. The year was 1964.

◆◆◆

"I FIRST HEARD ABOUT the Beatles on the news on our black and white TV," Allen told me. "Then they played *The Ed Sullivan Show* on that first Sunday in February and it really was as powerful as they say. Right then I knew I would learn how to play guitar and be in a band. I was hooked."

That the Beatles were a catalyst for 20/20 should come as no surprise, but the young Allen already had plenty of other influences closer to home. His mother sang in a vocal duo in high school, and both of his parents frequented dances at Cain's Ballroom where famous Western Swing band Bob Wills and the Texas Playboys performed. His paternal grandmother was a part-time piano teacher, and his older cousin played guitar in an early sixties guitar group. It was the perfect Petri dish for a budding music lover.

But it was Allen's older sister Lana who really accelerated his learning curve, exposing him to local teen radio and the singles she bought. "I loved 'Telstar,' 'The Lion Sleeps Tonight,' 'Wipe Out,' and 'Tequila,'" Allen said. "I loved the 'Monster Mash' and the groove of that song. I later found out it was Earl Palmer on drums and Leon Russell on piano."

When it comes to legendary Oklahoma musicians, Russell (born Claude Russell Bridges in Lawton, Oklahoma) is right up there with stylistically diverse heavyweights like Woody Guthrie, Charlie Christian, Chet Baker, and J. J. Cale (Russell's former bandmate in the Starlighters). Russell was a celebrated multi-instrumentalist, songwriter, arranger, solo artist, and producer during his decades-long career, working with everybody from the Beach Boys, the Byrds and Badfinger to the Rolling Stones, Elton John, and the Flying Burrito Brothers. It was the Church Studio and Shelter Records, which Russell cofounded, that would later figure into 20/20's origin story. But let's not get ahead of ourselves…

The summer of sixty-four changed Allen's life in many ways. His family moved to a different neighborhood a few months before he started sixth grade and—most importantly—he scored his cousin's Silvertone guitar and matching amp as an eleventh birthday present. The gift was followed by lessons at a local music store where guitar legend (and future member of Merle Haggard's backing band, the Strangers) Eldon Shamblin became Allen's teacher and mentor.

Allen also met Ron Flynt around the neighborhood that summer. The two immediately bonded over baseball and music, and the seeds of 20/20 were sown. "Our moms started talking and both found out we were learning guitar so they arranged for us to get together and play. How cool looking back. I could play chords and Ron could play melody," Allen said. "We were on our way. Spending the night, watching Beatles cartoons in the morning, and trying to learn how to make music. That just continued on and on through the years."

Like Allen, Flynt's life was changed by seeing the Beatles perform on TV that year. His father was an engineer while his mother stayed home to take care of him and his two siblings. Flynt's early exposure to music came in the form of Southern Baptist hymnals and gospel music. He played a little piano at church, getting his first guitar when he was ten. "I switched to bass after Steve and I started playing together. I got a Vox Panther bass and a little Rickenbacker amp," Flynt said.

The duo immediately cowrote songs (fitting that a couple of future power pop legends named their first effort "Girlfriend"), quickly making their world debut at a backyard birthday party. It wasn't long before they started putting groups together and performing at the many "Battle of the Bands" competitions springing up around Tulsa in the wake of Beatlemania. Allen still has a program from when their quintet, the Recount Four, played "The Last Time" by the Rolling Stones and "Money" by the Beatles at the Skelly Junior High School talent show. Their loss to the New Rivieras thankfully didn't deter Allen and Flynt from pursuing a career in music.

Flynt's uncle recorded the young band doing "You Better Run" by the Young Rascals and an instrumental version of "Music to Watch Girls By" by the Bob Crewe Generation. They submitted the tracks to a local lip-synch TV show called *Dance Party*, securing a coveted spot (and getting their first taste of band drama when their drummer refused to wear the puffy shirts the band picked out; they settled for matching jackets and dickies instead).

"In middle school and high school, we mostly played gyms, sock hops, and battles of the bands in National Guard armories," Flynt said. They eventually graduated to bars and clubs under revolving band names with various configurations while attending Oklahoma State University in nearby Stillwater. That's when Allen first stumbled on a flourishing scene of like-minded local musicians that focused his energy.

"I was sitting in Bill's Italian Restaurant and they had the little jukebox ports on each table. There was this song called 'I'm On Fire,'" Allen said. "I later saw the Dwight Twilley Band on *American Bandstand* and it was a real shot of competition and ambition. It was fucking cool, and they were on Shelter Records to boot."

Flynt agrees. "'I'm On Fire' made a big impact on me because at the time there were not many hits on the radio that sounded like that. Also, they were from Tulsa, just like us."

Sensing the possibilities, Allen submitted a single by his band Sweet Virginia—Flynt also eventually joined the band—to Shelter Records. He was invited down to the Church Studio for a meeting with the label's A&R rep, Simon Miller-Mundy. The meeting coincided with a recording session for a new Florida group called Mudcrutch. The band's lead singer, Tom Petty, played their first single for Allen, who thought "they sounded like Van Morrison." Allen also connected with future collaborator Phil Seymour through the Church Studio around the same time.

Seymour is a power pop legend in his own right. He was a multi-instrumentalist, vocalist, and founding member of the Dwight Twilley Band, recording two albums with the group before going solo. He also famously sang backing vocals on "American Girl" and "Breakdown" for Tom Petty and the Heartbreakers. A couple of Seymour's best-known solo songs include "Precious to Me" and "Baby It's You."

Allen didn't end up with a record deal from Shelter, but he'd caught a glimpse of rock stardom and made some serious connections. Armed with an exciting new batch of songs (influenced by everybody from the Beatles and Raspberries to Slade, T. Rex, and Roxy Music) he dropped out of college and headed for Los Angeles. Allen briefly returned to Oklahoma that Christmas to record a few eight-track demos with Flynt and Seymour before heading west for good. Flynt followed six months later, after graduating with a music degree. Allen already had a drummer, Mike Gallo, and a band name when Flynt arrived.

◆◆◆

20/20 WOODSHEDDED FOR A year before making their LA debut. The trio featured Allen on guitar/vocals, Flynt on bass/vocals, and Gallo on drums. They rented space at a cheap, rat-infested studio where they could turn up the volume to rehearse for a slew of upcoming gigs around town. "The club scene was fantastic when I first got to LA. There were so many good bands and an inspired DIY aspect to the scene that was cool," Flynt said.

The band completed the demos Allen and Flynt recorded back in Oklahoma, adding guitar and vocals at LA's famed United Western Studios (thanks to another Oklahoma friend who worked there). Greg Shaw from Bomp! Records agreed to release two of those songs, "Giving It All" backed with "Under The Freeway," as their debut single. That's when the steady whirlwind of activity spun into a Midwestern tornado.

"Shaw wanted us to put out an album, but we wanted to see if we could get a major label deal. I'm so glad we did. We kept writing and a Tuesday-night residency at Madame Wong's landed us an *LA Times* story. That's when it all turned into a music business fast-track that swept us off our feet," Allen said. "I think we started playing around in 1978. The *LA Times* article came out in January 1979."

Chris Silagyi was added on keyboards around this time "to get a bigger sound," according to Allen. The band continued writing, recording demos, and slugging it out in LA clubs. The hard work and major label gamble paid off when 20/20 signed with Portrait Records (Epic/CBS) a few months later. They were cutting basic tracks with producer Earle Mankey by June; that same month, the Knack took power pop into the top ten with "My Sharona." 20/20 couldn't have asked for a more receptive music market than the one they were entering.

"We made the first record at Sound City. We'd drive out there in the late afternoon and drive back into Hollywood early in the morning after having recorded all night. I really loved those drives. We'd talk about the record, girls, movies; it was fun being in a band and doing something important," Flynt said.

It was during the album sessions that Phil Seymour briefly came back into the fold. The decision was made to bring in a session drummer, and their old Oklahoma collaborator was the perfect fit (although Mike Gallo did play on "Tell Me Why (Can't You Understand)" according to Allen; and Gallo gets songwriting credit for that one and "Jet Lag"). "Mike had written great drum parts, which we had performed over and over again getting them to that state. I remember Phil saying to me, 'I'm just playing Mike's drum parts,'" Allen said. "Mike had tons of creative energy that helped 20/20 in every direction."

With an updated studio rhythm section in place, *20/20* was tracked and mixed in less than a month. "Yellow Pills" might not have been the first single, but it was the lead-off track (excluding the 1:13 sound collage called "The Sky Is Falling 7/79"—written by Silagyi—that opens side one).

Allen wrote 20/20's power pop "hit" shortly before they went into the studio with Mankey. He maintains that the song's name-sake tablets were never intended to represent any specific drug, but more the zeitgeist of the moment. The remarkably timeless lyrics manage to celebrate the birth of a hip new scene while simultaneously sending it up (has the word "groovy" ever felt so loaded?), all in an ultra-modern style laced with sixties psychedelia.

All of those elements make "Yellow Pills" the quintessential power pop song, but perhaps only in retrospect. When pressed by Dick Clark to describe 20/20's music—between energetic performances of "Remember the Lightning" and "Yellow Pills" on *American Bandstand*—Allen goes with "new music," "new pop," and "third generation rock" over "power pop." These days, Allen is even more abstract when describing the beloved track. "All I know is when I heard it loud at Sound City, through those big speakers, it sounded like German Expressionism to me."

20/20 was released in October 1979. Several songs from the album were starting to get airplay on LA tastemaker FM stations like KROQ and KLOS, according to Allen, who remembers "Yellow Pills" quickly emerging as an early favorite. "I'd be getting into my car outside the Hollywood apartment where I wrote ['Yellow Pills'] and hear it on the radio. It was an insane rock fantasy come to life."

Everything was going 20/20's way. Allen and Flynt recruited Joel Turrisi on drums for the touring band. They hit the road, headlining clubs across the US with occasional dates supporting the Ramones, Joe Jackson, and Hall & Oates. Forty years later it's the New York shows that still stand out for Allen, including a gig at Hurrah where they met ukulele-strumming art rock hero Tiny Tim; and a new wave show at the Palladium (also featuring power pop legends the Beat) where Andy Warhol hung out backstage. But one of Allen's biggest touring highlights was Mick Jagger watching from the side of the stage as 20/20 played "Yellow Pills."

It must have been a surreal moment for Allen and Flynt, a couple of elementary-school friends who first bonded over British Invasion bands. But their perfect night onstage in New York came to an end, just like their perfect debut album eventually ran its course. Four decades later, it's still hard for fans (myself included) to believe that the "Tell Me Why (Can't You Understand)" backed with "Yellow Pills" single never charted; the same is true for the unbelievable follow-up single, "Cheri" backed with "Backyard Guys." *20/20* peaked at 138 on the Billboard 200—an impressive debut, but not a hit record by major label standards. It was time to write new songs for a follow-up album.

Their sophomore effort, 1981's *Look Out!* (Portrait Records), is a decidedly more post-punk collection. Turrisi was now a full-time member of the band and his more aggressive drumming gives 20/20's pop sound a pronounced edge. Standout tracks include "Nuclear Boy" with its unbelievably hooky chorus (and further nods to New York–era Mick Jagger with the dual vocal pronunciation of "about you" as "about-CHOO!"); the sneering Clash-meets-Jam energy of "Life In The USA"; and the driving, angular urgency of Silagyi's "Beat City." The band parted ways with Portrait after *Look Out!*, releasing their third album, *Sex Trap* (Mainway Records), with Dean Korth on drums in 1982. (*Sex Trap* was rereleased a year later on Enigma Records). But those albums deserve their own essay.

For now, let's leave Allen and Flynt back where we found them, at the tail end of *20/20*'s promotional cycle. "That tour came to an end right before Christmas. The tour manager was a New Yorker who kept talking about all the 'podunk towns' we drove through. He was driving us home to visit family and sure enough he got quiet as we exited the freeway to drop us off in podunk Oklahoma," Allen recalls. "We were exhausted and weary, but ready for more rock and roll glory."

It's a pure high many of us—fans and musicians alike—will chase forever.

S. W. Lauden *is the author of the Greg Salem punk rock PI series including* Bad Citizen Corporation, Grizzly Season, *and* Hang Time. *His power pop–themed crime novelettes include* That'll Be The Day: A Power Pop Heist *and* Good Girls Don't: A Second Power Pop Heist. *S. W. Lauden is the pen name of Steve Coulter, drummer from Tsar and the Brothers Steve.*

Perfect Vision: The Story Behind Power Pop's First Fanzine, Yellow Pills

By Jordan Oakes

IN THE EARLY NINETIES, those musically lonely years that bridged the "shoegazer" sound and the calculated ugliness of grunge, power pop fans were caught between rock and a hard place. It had been over ten years since skinny ties (which were more myth and metaphor than sartorial gospel) and major labels took the genre as close as it's ever gotten to mainstream. In the early nineties, it was peace and quiet on the music front, the cold war after the battle of the bands. There were bursts of power pop energy, like Material Issue, in the midst of the drone, but for the most part, power pop was a scarce commodity.

Yellow Pills began with a mission: to write exclusively about power pop; to connect the dots of fandom; and to interview the artists. Journalistically devoted to this well-loved but oft maligned and misunderstood genre, I attempted to fill a gap. There had been Greg Shaw's *Bomp! Magazine*, which, despite championing power pop, covered garage and punk with just as much fervor (albeit holistically guided by Shaw's larger-than-the-sum-of-its-parts vision). There was *CREEM*, which journaled much the same territory as *Bomp!* but with a bit more irreverence. *Trouser Press* and *NY Rocker* were seminal publications that influenced *Yellow Pills*, but neither, of course, had a strictly power pop agenda.

Yellow Pills set out to legitimize a style that had been almost reflexively dismissed by the era's "important" rock-critic cognoscenti. The first *Rolling Stone Record Guide*, for one, used a critical machete to slice through skinny ties as if they were obstructive vines in the rock and roll jungle. To be fair, *Rolling Stone's* Dave Marsh was an admitted Raspberries fan (perhaps, speculates my inner cynic, because Springsteen was too?), and other reviewers, like Robert Christgau, made respectful and pithy observations about Shoes, Big Star, Artful Dodger, and the Scruffs. Still, in the annals of "serious" rock criticism, an unabashed appreciation for power pop was a rare thing. Full-blown journalistic respect and attention were yet to be expressed and articulated.

Yellow Pills, which I started with my friend Rich Osmond, came together at a strange moment in fanzine history—the cut-paste-and-staple days before most zines were designed on computer. We wrote it on a typewriter (until we got a word processor, the vegetable of computers), shrunk down four eight-by-eleven pages, scotch-taped them on a regular-sized sheet, and literally went to town on the xerox machine.

Many people reading this article already know the origin of the name, but let me recount: at least ten years earlier—around 1980—I had read about the SoCal-by-way-of-Tulsa power pop combo 20/20 in *Rolling Stone*. It was an article about the vibrant, then-current LA music scene of the Knack era—a time when numerous bands strove for success and legitimacy in the shadow of "My Sharona." I happened to find a promo of 20/20's eponymous debut LP in the "new wave" bin at my favorite record store. I was instantly in awe. The album fused a sense of post-teenage innocence with a strain of Hollywood depravity, of life caving in all around them (expressed succinctly on their second record's "Nuclear Boy"). This was a band to whom romance was merely the root of something more worldly and dangerous. 20/20 captured the confusion of love and its bitter aftertaste better than any group west of Shoes. And yet beneath the melodic sheen and layers of Beatlesque harmonies was a playful, get-up-and-jump rowdiness, even a smidge of rockabilly.

The first song on *20/20* (after a crashing sound effect track called "The Sky Is Falling") is an impressionistic whirl of neo-psychedelic pop-rock called "Yellow Pills," given a new-wave edge by expressive keyboards and Earl Mankey's shiny, pressure-cooked production. It felt like an anthem.

So 20/20 provided the answer to "what do we call this fanzine?" But the larger question of exactly what constitutes power pop has become oddly controversial—even confrontational—in recent years. Many fans cite a checklist of requisite attributes. I certainly have mine, which are nonetheless flexible: a solid melody presented in a rock setting that filters the sixties through the seventies; guitars that seamlessly exhibit strength and jangle; vocals, often fortified with harmonies, that get the passion across; bridges that burn into your brain; and choruses that rise above life's doldrums (never dull drums). And although, through the years, power pop has been remade and remodeled to assimilate with trends, sometimes hiding in odd musical places, it lives in its own anachronistic bubble. When you hear a power pop song, you know it.

Sometimes confirmation is after the fact.

In my formative years, I sought out the music as if my turntable depended on it. Who was Dwight Twilley? I did my research and found *Sincerely*—but not before I bought Phil Seymour's debut.

There were so many two and twos to put together. The summer of 1980 provided a crash course in cruising music. Because in many ways, that's what power pop was—even outside the literal drive of Raspberries' "Cruisin' Music." Many of the songs themselves were, in fact, very moving vehicles. I bought the double LP reissue of the Big Star albums, the first of which, to this day, never fails to make me cry. I discovered Shoes, dB's, and the Records. I was drawn to the springy art-beat of XTC. Every new band, from the button-down to the quirky and radical, seemed to fit into the larger picture—a jigsaw puzzle that I was putting together in the form of a record collection.

And a full decade later, I was putting my pop education to use. Not that "Let's Pretend" was our credo and philosophy, but *Yellow Pills* pretended to be a "real magazine." I tried to adhere to a self-imposed, one-issue-a-month schedule. We even took subscriptions, a deceptively complicated undertaking without a computer. We were the writers, the printers, the post office errand boys; we wore so many hats, people must have thought we were bald. Bold, perhaps.

We decided to put an iconic power pop band on the cover of each issue, beginning with Cheap Trick. Which was kind of fitting, because after immersing myself in the music of the Beatles in the late seventies, I took an immediate left turn into Cheap Trick. In fact, the first time I'd ever heard the term power pop was in reference to their *Dream Police* album. Through the course of the magazine's tenure, I managed to interview Paul Collins, Scott Miller, Dwight Twilley, Tommy Dunbar, Emitt Rhodes, Bill Lloyd, and countless others. I had always connected with their music. Now I was connecting with *them*.

Hitting its (relative) stride around 1992, *Yellow Pills* preceded the everybody-has-a-computer age, which not only meant I had to print it rudimentarily, but that the only way, up to this point, that fans of the genre could find and contact one another was by way of "snail mail" or telephone. They were people simply longing to pinch another power pop fan to make sure they were real. People from all corners of the world were sending me their demos, expressing gratitude that *Yellow Pills* existed.

My first letter ever was from Darian Sahanaja of the dreamy studio group called Wondermints. They were a bells-and-whistles, post-surf kind of combo with the best cassette demo I'd ever heard. They evoked post-1966 Beach Boys, perhaps, but not at the expense of their own soul—for example, not many bands could claim the simultaneous influence of Phil Spector, Elvis Costello, and prog. I reviewed their tape in one of the earliest issues. Wondermints embarked on a string of live shows in Los Angeles. In the audience one night was Brian Wilson. The rest is pretty much history, as Wondermints essentially became Wilson's new, de facto Beach Boys; and, as of this writing, continue to tour the world as his back-up band (although Wilson's lineup has changed from time to time, most notably after the untimely death of 'Mints guitarist Nick Walusko).

Though *Yellow Pills* was distributed directly from my calloused fingertips to subscribers' mailboxes, that one-man-operation aspect changed when a fanzine shop in Manhattan contacted me to get some copies. In weeks, they sold out of the first batch, so I kept replenishing. I began to hear from pop fans in Japan, France, England, Spain, and Australia. I realized the zine was playing a part in something bigger.

By the fourth issue, Rich Osmond decided to move on, having understandably grown weary of the fanzine conveyor belt. Rich had laid out the first few issues, and his love of pop-punk and eighties exploitation flicks had been a big part of the early

Yellow Pills. I soldiered on. One day I got a surprise call from a guy named Dean Brownrout, who had come across *Yellow Pills* in that New York zine shop. He expressed surprise and excitement at having discovered a fanzine devoted entirely to pop. His favorite band was Badfinger, he told me. He asked if I'd ever considered putting together a compilation of the sort of music covered in *Yellow Pills*. Brownrout had recently formed a record label called Big Deal, and wanted me to "executive produce" a power pop compilation for the label.

Excitedly, I got to work, and discovered it wasn't that difficult to track down the bands and artists on my wish list. That most weren't exactly superstars with a mansion on the hill helped immeasurably. Some had been through the usual getting-signed-and-underpromoted process of near misses and broken dreams. Others were up-and-comers, or obscurities I wanted to make known. In my eyes (and ears) they were all musical giants: the four-piece poets of my adolescence.

Before long I was being called—and we're talking landline here—by Dwight Twilley, Gary Klebe of Shoes, Matthew Sweet, Tommy Dunbar; you name it. Imagine that: They were calling me. They wanted to give me a song. And they were all good songs, of course, because along with being unfailingly talented, these bands wanted to put their best foot forward. Everything fell into place like a choreographed dance.

The first *Yellow Pills* CD garnered an astonishing amount of response. It was possibly the first CD compilation of 100 percent power pop, and that was its stated objective. I ended up putting together four CDs for Big Deal, which included the Plimsouls, Matthew Sweet, Gigolo Aunts, 20/20, Shoes, Twilley, the Loud Family, Andrew Gold, Redd Kross, and too many others to list in a paragraph. I felt so incredibly lucky. Unlike most compilations, the *Yellow Pills* CDs weren't made to promote a label or new albums by the included musicians. The songs were, in almost every case, previously unreleased. The CDs were self-contained, sequenced for maximum effect. And outside the small world of my typewriter, an excitement was brewing, most notably in Los Angeles, where a genre-celebrating music festival called Poptopia commenced. Celebrities showed up. Legendary venues like The Roxy and the Troubadour were booked with groups and artists I'd once only dreamt of seeing. The magazine felt connected to the burgeoning scene. Things had come full circle, too, as 20/20, who, for me, started it all, emerged from the same city's previous pop renaissance.

In the late nineties, I ceased publication of *Yellow Pills* as I felt that the CD series had usurped the magazine at that point, at least in terms of my devoted energy. After four CDs and nine issues, my verve for multitasking had been depleted. Life went on. One day, around the very beginning of the twenty-first century (just several years later, but it sounds cool to put it that way), I was contacted by another label to do a new *Yellow Pills* comp. I took the assignment. It turned out to be a double CD, and this time most of the bands contributed two or three songs as opposed to just one. I called it *Yellow Pills: Prefill*. While the Big Deal CDs seemed to emphasize the jangle end of the spectrum, *Prefill* homed in on the late seventies/early eighties sound, the era in which the bifurcation between punk and power pop blurred. As before, I chose all the songs, sequenced them, and wrote the liner notes. With the exception of an unreleased early seventies track by the band Artful Dodger (before they were Artful Dodger), *Prefill* more or less covered pop's second wave. This time the source was my own record collection; in fact, some tracks on the comp were mastered directly from my vinyl copies. Again, the response was positive and enthusiastic. I was floored to see *Prefill* reviewed in *Entertainment Weekly*. (Yes, that's my rusty mailbox on the CD cover.)

I look back at the years I worked on *Yellow Pills* and think about how fun it was to be a part of something I believed in, to keep the beach ball of power pop up in the air.

Jordan Oakes *founded, published, and edited the* Yellow Pills *power-pop magazine beginning in 1991, and compiled five Yellow Pills CD compilations beginning in 1993. His journalism has also appeared in* Sound Choice, Speak, The Riverfront Times, The Christian Science Monitor, Rolling Stone's "Alt-Rock-a-Rama" book, *and elsewhere. He's a published poet and occasional stand-up comedian. He loves dogs and dog-eared magazines.*

Los Anglophiles:
Jangly Pop Echoes in Distant Canyons

By Paul Myers

IN THE HORRIBLE SPRING of 2020, Los Angeles–based musician and songwriter Taylor Locke sent me a preview of something he was working on that would eventually be released on an EP entitled *The Bitter End*. This was immaculately played and sung melodic rock that seemed vestigially connected to both mid-sixties London and mid-seventies California while also evoking the nineties studio craft of Jellyfish and the post-grunge crunch of the Grays. Locke's guitar solos made nods to the same post-*Revolver* George Harrison bends favored by a Jon Brion or a Jason Falkner. The UK/LA personality of the music seemed of a piece with the celebrated Los Anglophiles of old, such as Harry Nilsson or the patron saint of home studio wizardry, Emitt Rhodes. There's something about British-rooted rock played by sun-drenched Los Angelinos, and ever since Roger McGuinn of the Byrds bought a twelve-string Rickenbacker after seeing *A Hard Day's Night*, a permanent British jangle has echoed through the canyons.

But Locke, formerly of the band Rooney and one-time touring member of LA's most English-sounding pop duo, Sparks, takes exception to what he sees as the "ghetto effect" implied by the term power pop, a label he sees as more often than not defined by outsider cult status.

"My pleasure lies in seeing supposed power pop bands *transcend* the 'secret society' of it and bring a broader cross section of fans to the party. My connection to this music comes from my love of its early iterations—the Who, Cheap Trick, Queen, Badfinger, Todd Rundgren—bands who actually *did* get played on the radio. I was in a band that were regarded as power pop, but we never used the term. To me, it was just melodic rock 'n' roll with curveball chord changes."

While I could relate to Locke's reluctance to join the outsider club, the very things I loved about his album were the sounds I identified with in the music of the Records, Big Star, and Badfinger; the sounds that led my nineties-era Toronto band, the Gravelberrys, to self-identify as power pop.

Many years later, I had moved to the Bay Area of Northern California and began to notice a hive of like-minded, pop-loving Los Angeles players showing up sporadically in places like the old Largo on Fairfax, where I had the privilege of opening a few Friday night shows for Jon Brion, who sometimes honored me by sitting in on a song. One night, I was even called up to play bass on Jon's cover of Badfinger's "No Matter What" backed by the Grays' drummer Dan McCarroll, jamming on Bowie's "Rebel Rebel" with Benmont Tench on the piano. Where else could you see Elliott Smith walk up to the side of the stage to pass a request note to Jon, who then proceeded to reinvent Cheap Trick's "Voices," loop upon loop, right before our very eyes, until it was some kind of art-rock beast?

My point of entry into the new LA pop subculture came in February of 2010, when I met Locke and Chris Price when their band, Taylor Locke and the Roughs, were opening a Sloan show in San Francisco. The following year, when my book *A Wizard A True Star: Todd Rundgren in the Studio* was published, I invited my new SoCal friends to join me in a musical joint book launch with Scott Miller's *Music: What Happened?* at Largo At the Coronet. That night, we assembled a fantastic lineup of pop-savvy LA musicians to play the show, including Lyle Workman, D. J. Bonebrake, Jon Brion, Mike Viola, the Section string quartet, and Aimee Mann, who even sang a duet with Scott. So many musical rivers crossed that night.

Then, a few years later, when Price was producing Emitt Rhodes' comeback album, *Rainbow Ends,* I flew down to Rhodes' fabled Hawthorne studio to cover the session for *Mojo Magazine.* While I was there, I was invited to sing on his cover of "How Can You Mend a Broken Heart" for the Bee Gees tribute album, *To Love The Bee Gees: A Tribute to the Brothers Gibb.* That one session introduced me to even *more* like-minded musicians such as Alex Jules, Emeen Zarookian, and Benjamin LeCourt, who later formed the group Bebopalula with Price right after coalescing on the Rhodes' record.

It was a very LA meeting, particularly because every one of these guys had come to LA from somewhere else. Price swept in from Miami, Zarookian hailed from Boston, LeCourt came from Paris, and Jules made his way west from New York.

But no matter where they came from, they all ended up crossing paths in LA. It all reminded me of the migration made by the late, great publicist Derek Taylor, who left his job with the Beatles in 1965 to go work for the Byrds on the Sunset Strip. I was so intrigued by this connection that I asked a few of these musicians just what it is about LA that makes it such a magnet for Anglophile pop lovers.

Chris Price notes that both geographically and musically, musicians and songwriters have been drawn to LA for the creative and commercial opportunities it affords them and the chance to follow in the footsteps of legends like Randy Newman and Harry Nilsson, or the Laurel Canyon and Hawthorne legends. In his opinion this makes for a "strange brew of commerce and art" that is unique to the City of Angels, where a continuum of ambitious and talented people can find that "sweet spot where uncompromised, challenging art is able to reach the masses."

"In my experience, the more you go out and make things, the more you find yourself presented with opportunities to make things," says Price. "I've certainly met lots of like-minded musicians playing on Tuesday nights at the jam in the Kibitz Room at Canter's Deli, as well as through the annual Wild Honey Orchestra shows that I've been involved in for the last six years or so. I met Alex Jules because we shared a bill together during the International Pop Overthrow festival."

On a personal note, Price notes that the Wondermints and their subsequent work with Brian Wilson presented a model for how to both make great contemporary music, and how to have a meaningful musical conversation with previous generations, such as his own work with Rhodes.

"I have certainly been influenced heavily by both of those crews," says Price, "and we even invited some of those people to collaborate on *Rainbow Ends*. I feel that all of us are on a chain together and the links should be talking as much as possible. I find myself extremely humbled and inspired by those around me."

Locke reckons that, regardless of the label, power pop's particular blend of the bitter and the sweet, the harmonious and melancholy, is very much like LA itself.

"Here we have the sunshine, beaches, the hills, the studios, and the superstars," says Locke, "and yet, just below the surface we've got millions of would-be artists, trying to get into the party. It's the land of folks with stars in their eyes who never got the lucky break or didn't have the goods they thought they did. Great talent and great success don't always come hand in hand, and so LA is host to both glamor and bitterness."

The Wondermints' Darian Sahanaja is one of the main players in Brian Wilson's current band, and even played with the Zombies on their *Odyssey and Oracle* tour. He points out that one of the more insidious influences of the Fab Four, particularly in the LA scene, is that it transcends genre.

"Every musician I've ever clicked with here has a deep appreciation for the Beatles," says Sahanaja. "The invasion they spearheaded in the sixties has been and continues to be an inspiration. I suppose it's rock 'n' roll filtered through the British experience that expanded the landscape. It gave us the first American garage-band movement, baroque pop, barrelhouse, Indian modal, and so on. While touring with the Zombies I'd bring this up with Rod Argent and he'd go on and describe how he simply didn't see any difference between the joys he'd experienced from listening to Bach and Miles Davis records to hearing Elvis on the radio. I think that kind of nondiscriminating appreciation in music was key to the evolution of pop in the late sixties."

Sahanaja gets a similar feeling from Brian Wilson, whom he commends for not being "bogged down by musical confines."

"And, of course, Brian was also heavily inspired by the Beatles," says Sahanaja. "He recognized the innovative song craft and it definitely made him up his game."

New Yorker Alex Jules came to LA to work with Price on his solo album *Topiary*, armed with a "Things To Do" list that included "find Emitt Rhodes and work with him." It didn't take long to realize that dream.

"Just as Chris and I were starting our preproduction work," says Jules, "he asked if I could do a session the following day. It turned out to be a session with Emitt. It felt especially fortuitous because that was also where I met the other members of Bebopalula. Emeen and I hit it off, then we went to a Bambi Kino gig, where I hit it off with Erik Paparozzi. A few months later, Erik asked me if I was available to sub on a Denny Laine show, a job I've had ever since. That led to playing with Chad & Jeremy, and then with Joey Molland. Bebopalula became a part of the Wild Honey family where we met Brian Wilson's band and performed with legends like Al Jardine, Garth Hudson, Jackson Browne, and John Sebastian. That led to me auditioning for the Monkees in early 2018, and then backing Nez on a tour with his First National Band. All of this, from loving the Beatles, which put me in a room with my entire future back at Emitt Rhodes' studio."

New Jersey–born Erik Paparozzi had always been drawn to the sound of LA and concurs with Sahanaja that the Beatles legend looms large in the scene. From there, he says, it's all the usual suspects.

"The night I met Emeen," says Paparozzi, "we went into my studio and played all of *Ram* from start to finish. And I've had many Jellyfish and Nilsson listening parties with Chris Price. I met Ben LeCourt at a Love Revisited show, and Love's *Forever Changes* is a huge record for me. When I started having bands in the nineties I always got the best reaction to my weirdo take on power pop when I came through LA, more so than other cities. That got me digging into Jon Brion, Jason Faulkner, Elliot Smith, and the 88, who really embodied that LA sound via British Invasion."

Boston-born Emeen Zarookian had fond childhood memories of visiting extended family members in LA, and always found it "colorful and exciting."

"I loved the Boston music scene," says Zarookian, "but I felt like I'd taken my music as far as it could go there. I had fans in Boston, but I felt like overall the genre wasn't super appreciated there, and artists/music/venues just weren't respected enough. So I came to LA to tap into the scene, which pretty much happened immediately when I got called in to work with Emitt."

Paparozzi has found that playing every night with pop legends like Denny Laine and Joey Molland is like entering a portal into his record collection and getting a master class in songwriting and arranging.

"They both still have all their power pop chops," says Paparozzi, "and they are incredibly adept at doling out intricate harmonies. And, of course, these guys have both made some of the classic power pop albums."

While Paparozzi pops up in the Laurel Canyon documentary *Echo in the Canyon*, one of its key players is Fernando Perdomo, who appears throughout the film as part of Jakob Dylan's house band. Now an established LA pop (and prog) producer and multi-instrumentalist, Perdomo had followed his friend Price out west from Miami to live the Hollywood dream.

"If you are a musician who loves power pop," says Perdomo, "LA is your mecca. The excitement when you find others as obsessed with the music as you are is amazing, and LA power pop was the biggest boom of power pop since the Beatles. From the Knack through to the Go-Go's, the Bangles—the nineties power pop explosion was just as mythical to us as the Beatles were. They had Abbey Road, we had Ocean Way, Capitol, and, of course, Emitt's garage."

PAUL MYERS

Perdomo's mecca analogy is particularly apt in the case of Irish pop maestro Thomas Walsh, leader of the Irish group Pugwash, who traveled all the way from Dublin to LA to record his group's *Silverlake* album with Jason Falkner in April of 2017.

"My love of LA was for the shimmering Santa Ana windswept pop of Michael Penn, Jellyfish, Jason Falkner, the Grays, and many others," says Walsh. "As a working-class Irishman from drizzle-loving Dublin it was like an untouchable world."

Having witnessed the journeys of England's XTC, who came to LA in 1988 to record their album *Orange & Lemons,* or fellow Irishmen, the Thrills, who recorded their own ode to California, *So Much For The City,* there in 2003, Walsh found his own pilgrimage clarifying.

"*Oranges & Lemons* is the Bible for us blow-ins to come over to LA and steal your sunshine and have sex with your Mellotrons," says Walsh. "Having been in LA many times now, that XTC masterpiece makes even more sunny sense than ever before. With *Silverlake* I did try and make my *Oranges & Lemons* and I think we made a decent little LA record which I'm very proud of; think of it as our 'Satsuma & Vinegar,' if you will."

LeCourt came all the way from France to be a part of the LA community, and says he enjoys feeling connected to the lineage of generations of musicians who, like himself, have come from all over the world to record there.

"Bebopalula was born out of the synergy generated by a common passion, and the desire to create something of our own," says LeCourt. "I don't think anybody can create anything new or fresh if they don't know about what happened before. And still, you have to find your own voice, your own stories to tell. Otherwise you would end up doing what we call in French '*un exercice de style,*' which means executing something in the style of. This could result in being very sterile and it doesn't bring anything interesting to the table."

LeCourt enjoys being part of the family tree that includes branches of such Jellyfish/Grays types as Brion and Falkner, Roger Joseph Manning Jr., or the Wondermints/Brian Wilson crew. He also points out that the line between LA power pop and the so-called Paisley Underground scene is a blurry one.

"I mean, Jason [Falkner] started in the Three O'Clock, and when I think jangly LA power pop, the Bangles are totally part of that lineage as well. Hawthorne has been home at some point to Debbie Harry, Emitt Rhodes, the Wilson family, and even Redd Kross, so it is fertile ground indeed. This city is a melting pot of influences with a long musical history. Bands from the sixties planted the seeds here, but the ample sunshine allows us to grow some great hooks, yet it's just urban enough to grow some pumping beats underneath it all."

It's the same beat that even drew a Canadian like me, born of Liverpool parents, to heed the call of that great poet of LA pop, Van Dyke Parks, to "Come to the Sunshine" and water the tree of California pop from time to time with my own Beatles-adjacent blood.

Pop on, Los Anglophiles; long may your fab jangle echo through the canyons.

Paul Myers *is a Canadian writer and musician based in Northern California. His writing has appeared in* Mojo *magazine and numerous other music journalism sites and periodicals. He is the author of four books, including* A Wizard a True Star: Todd Rundgren in the Studio *and* Kids in the Hall: One Dumb Guy. *His short memoir,* The Cherokee Record Club, *appeared in Rare Bird's 2013 prog rock anthology,* Yes Is The Answer. *He is currently the host and producer of* The Record Store Day Podcast.

Into the Arena

By Doug Brod

The MetroCentre in Rockford, Illinois. New Year's Eve, 1982.

IT's THE THIRD NIGHT of KISS's tour supporting *Creatures of the Night*, their tenth studio album and arguably their heaviest to date. It's also their third night performing with Vinnie Vincent, who replaced lead guitarist Ace Frehley most everywhere on the album except the cover. The band, celebrating their tenth anniversary, may have scaled down their theatrics slightly for this go-around, but their stage set, designed to resemble a tank, still includes a drum riser on a turret with a phallic love gun aimed directly at the crowd.

For the first few shows of the tour, before either Night Ranger or the Plasmatics would join as main support, KISS have enlisted as opening bands little-known regional groups: Hotz in North Dakota, Dare Force in Iowa, Why on Earth in Indiana, and the Defectors in West Virginia. Tonight, a decidedly better-known (but not to this crowd) band got the nod. And from the looks of them, they are the anti-KISS—no, not Angel, but really the opposite of KISS, four guys from nearby Zion, Illinois, clad conservatively in dress shirts or tees, jeans or corduroys. There is absolutely nothing hard-rocking about this band called Shoes and seemingly nothing tying them to KISS, except for the fact that bassist Gene Simmons adores them.

This wouldn't be the first time a band branded "power pop" opened for the grease-painted, blood-spitting rock specters. On New Year's Eve in 1974, Raspberries shared a bill with KISS, as did Pezband a few months later. So did Graham Parker & the Rumour in November 1976. And mostly due to Simmons' patronage, Cheap Trick famously supported KISS on an arena tour in 1977, which was crucial to exposing that young band to an audience beyond their Midwest club diehards.

There were few chances in the mid- and late seventies for skinny-tied, middle-parted purveyors of melodic pop rock to perform live outside a bar, club, or theater, save for a multiband bill at a Summerfest or some such. "In 1979, it was still early for anything new to penetrate the mainstream," says Brad Steakley, whose power pop–leaning Screams opened for Van Halen that year. "People still wanted to hear Ted Nugent, Peter Frampton, Bad Company, and Aerosmith." It wasn't until the early eighties that the Police made it safe to sport blazers and Capezios in a stadium.

Creatures of the Night was seen as a return to KISS's hard-rock roots after detours into disco (*Dynasty*), new-wavey pop (*Unmasked*), and proggy pretension (*Music from "The Elder"*). But the band's fortunes had taken a downturn and the tour featured two unfamiliar new members (the other was drummer Eric Carr), so the turnout tonight is, perhaps predictably, lousy: 3,500 in a venue that holds more than 9,000.

For Shoes, this marks their first time playing an arena. (They'd open for the Kinks at Chicago's UIC Pavilion the following year.) The band already had a connection to KISS when they were booked for the show: Mike Stone, who produced their first album for Elektra, had worked on KISS's greatest-hits collection *Double Platinum* and engineered Gene Simmons's 1978 solo album. When Shoes were recording with Stone, they'd heard that at one point Simmons declared them his favorite group. While Shoes shared Simmons's love of sixties pop and the British Invasion, they were less enamored of his band. "We definitely were not KISS fans," says singer-guitarist Gary Klebe. "It was pretty far from our focus."

But they did see an opportunity. "We've always said, 'Is it better to play for a hundred of your fans as opposed to 2,000 that don't know you?'" says bassist-singer John Murphy.

Admitting that they looked like they could have been anybody off the street, Shoes were surprised by the reception. "We thought we were going to get pelted up there," Klebe says, "but it wasn't that way at all." It helped that they came prepared, tailoring their set to a tight forty minutes of their more raucous material.

"We knocked out anything that wasn't *bam, bam!*" says Murphy. "We just hit them with our version of hard stuff"—songs like "Burned Out Love," "Too Late," "Tomorrow Night," "Mayday," "Curiosity," and "In Her Shadow." The crowd may have greeted each song with mild, polite applause, but the band still heard scattered catcalls. "We probably got fewer 'Shoes suck!' than we do at a regular Shoes show," Klebe says with a laugh.

After their set, from the back of the arena, Shoes watched and enjoyed the headliner's spectacle, which was the first KISS show for each of them. "And last," adds Murphy. But it wouldn't be their final contact with Simmons. Impressed by a review he'd seen of *Shoes Best*, in early 1988 the budding entrepreneur tracked the band down and offered to manage them and sign them to his new Simmons Records imprint. They came close to doing a deal,

Klebe says, "but we just couldn't get it together in the end to make him happy [enough] to move forward."

For all their bluster and bombast, KISS themselves had a history of dabbling in power pop (see "Comin' Home," "Let Me Know," "Anything for My Baby," and Simmons and Stanley's 1978 solo joints), so it wasn't that unusual when KISS took on tour two bands from the crunchier end of genre's spectrum. The first, Artful Dodger, was a quintet from outside Washington, DC, managed by Steve Leber and David Krebs, who also counted Aerosmith and Ted Nugent among their charges. The band's first album for Columbia, in 1976, featured the minor classic "Wayside," which gained a second life on a 1993 *Come Out and Play* compilation from Rhino. As with so many bands of the era, for whom it was determined that prolificity was the key to success and cash flow, Artful Dodger felt pressure from management to quickly record a follow-up. When Jack Douglas, who produced their debut and had worked with Aerosmith but not yet with Cheap Trick, was unavailable, his associate Eddie Leonetti got the assignment.

The group had already appeared on bills with the likes of Blue Öyster Cult and Ted Nugent when, in July 1976, they played the first of sixteen shows on the Destroyer tour. Though Artful Dodger hit it off with the members of KISS, guitarist Gary Herrewig told *Goldmine* in 2010 that the audiences shunned them. "We were just too drastically different," he said, adding that his band should have ditched the tour and instead waited until Douglas was free to work on their second record. That album, *Honor Among Thieves*, which disappointed the group, is actually a terrific effort, highlighted by the gritty, swaggering title track and a hypnotically howling cover of Little Richard's "Keep A-Knockin.'"

Back then, competing management companies would often trade opening acts to tour with their bigger bands, so KISS's Bill

Aucoin would take out an Artful Dodger, say, and Leber-Krebs would let Aucoin's Starz support Aerosmith. "You went into a 12,000-seat arena," says Krebs, who loved Artful Dodger and brought them into the fold, "and at the end of the opening act's show, it was very much like the Colosseum in Rome with the thumbs up or down."

In hindsight, his former partner Leber says the problem was that while the likes of AC/DC and Aerosmith worked bars forever, if a band didn't have the ability to attract crowds in their hometown, they were doomed. "Artful Dodger wasn't drawing anybody," he says. "We built our business on groups that had emerged already as local rock-and-roll superstars. All these other groups didn't have years of experience being bar bands."

Bill Aucoin kept it in the family when his band Piper, led by Billy Squier, opened eight dates for KISS in late 1977. The three-guitar group, signed to A&M, released a fine self-titled debut earlier that year, highlighted by a rollicking cover of the Rolling Stones' "Last Time," featuring a slide guitar that makes it sound like the Monkees taking the last train to Clarksville, and "Who's Your Boyfriend? (I Got a Feelin')," a chunk of delicious bubble glam that Squier later redid, to marvelous effect, on his 1980 solo debut, *Tale of the Tape*.

But it was on *Can't Wait*, Piper's second album, also from 1977, where the band blossomed. As evidenced by the magnificent title track, hooky "Drop By and Stay," proto pop-punk "Bad Boy," and stirring "Now Ain't the Time"—on which he nicked the melody line from "Only Love Can Break Your Heart" for a country waltz that climaxes in an impassioned gospel plea—Squier took a purer, single-centric approach to songwriting. The record's true stunner, "See Me Through," sounds like the Led Zeppelin of "Over the Hills and Far Away," covering a lost Big Star B-side. And according to drummer Richie Fontana, that one, preposterously, never got an airing in concert.

"We really nailed it on that album," says Fontana, adding that Aucoin's lover and creative guru Sean Delaney, who coproduced with Stones man Chris Kimsey, was instrumental in prepping Piper's stage show. The band had done a bunch of support spots with Uriah Heap and ZZ Top, but aesthetically their pairings with ELO, Angel, and the Babys seemed to make a lot more sense.

"KISS requested we open for them," says Fontana, recalling that his band went over so well that they got an encore at Madison Square Garden in their home base of New York City. Alas, they didn't last long when the second album failed to make an impact. After leaving A&M, Piper spilt, with guitarist Alan Nolan gravitating toward the CBGB scene and Aucoin pushing Squier toward a solo career. For his part, Fontana later drummed on nearly half of Paul Stanley's 1978 solo LP, including "Wouldn't You Like to Know Me," as gloriously catchy a song as the KISS coleader has recorded.

When they opened a whopping forty-four dates on Van Halen's first headlining tour, Screams had an experience similar to Piper's. They were a hard-to-categorize anomaly; influenced by the Who, David Bowie, Sparks, and the Sex Pistols, they pledged allegiance to no genre. They did, however, build a reputation based on their live and sonic resemblance to one of the hottest new acts of the time.

"I think we were one of the very first, if not the first, Midwest bands that jumped on the Cheap Trick thing," says Brad Steakley, who as Brad Elvis would later drum for the Elvis Brothers and the Romantics. "We used to see them in the clubs. We got to see it live and learn from it." After a showcase for the just-formed Infinity Records label at the Manhattan club Trax in early December

1978, they signed a deal. Around three weeks later, they flew to Sausalito, California, to cut their debut at the Record Plant. The self-titled result, released the following May, is something of a minor masterpiece, packed with sturdy, inordinately tuneful songs with an acidic tang. Buzzing power chords and Steakley's frenetic fills punctuate "Paper Dolls," which resolves in a repetitive chant of "all right" that's clearly an homage to Rick Nielsen and co. On "Angeline's Toys," driven by Steven Jones' meaty bass, singer David Adams does his best approximation of Robin Zander's desperate bellow. "It's Just a Matter of Time," "Your Girl, My Girl," and "Financial Disaster (It's Only Money)" also capture the Cheap Trick vibe, with the last one mastering their use of whiny backup singing to offset otherwise tough lead vocals. On the solemn "Pop Art," despite a lyrical shoutout to Marc Bolan, Adams tries on Bowie's Thin White croon—and it's an elegant fit.

For Screams, it came as a shock when their booking agent snagged them the 1979 Van Halen shows, from July (just two months after the debut's release) through October. Echoing Shoes, they didn't care much for the headliners. "We're like, 'Really, Van Halen? *Ucch*,'" Steakley says. "'Why can't it be somebody cool like Cheap Trick?'"

They had already played good-sized halls with the mismatched likes of REO Speedwagon, the Guess Who, and Head East, as well as smaller venues with the more likeminded Ramones, Iggy Pop, and the Atlantics. "Blondie, Talking Heads, Ramones— they weren't playing big places, so you didn't really have a lot of choices," Steakley says, which is why touring 5,000-plus-capacity venues with the country's up-and-comingest hard-rock band might not have been a bad idea. "And we did really well at every gig. We held our own."

It may have helped that while he was like Keith Moon back there attacking his kit, Jones pounded his bass like he was in Deep Purple, Adams strutted around swinging his mic, and guitarist John Siegle leapt around bashing out distorted leads.

It certainly didn't hurt that Van Halen liked them. Steakley remembers once helping Alex Van Halen calibrate his drums. "A road guy usually does it," he says, "but no one ever hits a drum right like a drummer. They just *tap, tap*." He also recalls sitting on the floor in a hotel room with Eddie Van Halen at a party in Canada, bonding over the Beatles. One of the few times he interacted with David Lee Roth was at a strip club on Sunset Boulevard after their final concert at the LA Forum. "He was sitting at a table, leaned back, and said, 'Hey, you guys, thanks a lot,'" says Steakley. "I'm like, 'Oh, you're welcome.' 'You got a light?' 'No.' He goes, 'Okay,' and turns around."

Not much later, Screams were playing a sold-out show at the Marquee Club in London when they got word that the plug was being pulled on Infinity, which had invested unwisely on a flop album of songs and speeches by Pope John Paul II. They flew home the next day without a deal, played for another year, and, says Steakley, amassed more than three albums' worth of "really cool songs that no one'll hear."

But for a band with modest beginnings in small-town Pekin, Illinois, the Van Halen tour afforded a taste of the rock-and-roll life they had always dreamed about. "It was a lot of deli trays," Steakley says, "but we had a big tour bus and everything. It was the seventies. It was the real deal."

Doug Brod *is the former editor in chief of SPIN and the author of* They Just Seem a Little Weird: How KISS, Cheap Trick, Aerosmith, and Starz Remade Rock and Roll. *He has written for* The New York Times, Billboard, Classic Rock, *and* The Trouser Press Record Guide, *among many other publications. A native New Yorker, he lives with his family in Toronto.*

Pop Snaps

By Tom Gracyk

IN 1976, I WAS flunking out of my engineering studies at the University of California, Davis. To salvage my college career, I switched over to the freewheeling classes in the design department. I bought a 35mm camera for an intro to photography class and learned the basics. Once I located a sympathetic teacher who would sign me up for Independent Studies and meet with me once a week to look at some photos, I had full access to the campus darkroom.

I now had a lot more free time to indulge my interest in music. I had been an avid listener since the age of ten, growing up just outside the San Francisco Bay Area listening at first to KFRC and KYA on the AM dial, and later to KSAN on the FM dial.

I knew from reading *Creem* and *Rolling Stone* that music reviewers got free records, but I didn't think that the *Cal Aggie* would be interested in running anything that I wanted to write about. There was a free community newspaper in Davis that took me on as a weekly contributor, but I couldn't figure out how to get any free records. I did review some concerts that I got into for free and interviewed some interesting musicians like Anthony Braxton and Robbie Basho.

Six months later, armed with my press clippings, I met with the arts editor of the *Cal Aggie* and offered him my services. He glanced at my work and said sure, if I wanted to write any records reviews, there's the box of new records that had come in that week. Goldmine!

I wasn't one of those guys who carried his camera with him wherever he went (although some teachers recommended it), but I took my camera to some concerts I reviewed. The Aggie ran my live photo of the Jam alongside my review—my first photo credit!

Soon my attention turned to KDVS-FM, the campus radio station. I met some older guys who had a late-night jazz show and seemed intrigued that I knew about modern jazz *and* modern rock, like the Ramones and Pere Ubu. They showed me the ropes and I signed up for a beginner's slot at the station, a weekly 2:00– 6:00 a.m. shift. The program director liked my style and mix so much that he moved me up to a prime 6:00–10:00 p.m. spot the following quarter.

I impressed the station's board with my enthusiasm and wide range of musical interest and became music director in the summer of 1978. My fellow DJs Russ Tolman (True West) and Steve Wynn (The Dream Syndicate)—both starting their musical careers around that time while matriculating at UC Davis—were the program directors, scheduling the jocks while I vetted the new music available for airplay. KDVS was the rare college station with 5000 watts of power (transmitting into parts of Sacramento), so we got plenty of attention from record labels and concert promoters.

In the late seventies the concert schedule at the UC Davis Coffee House exploded and I was the liaison working with the promo people to get their touring acts exposure on KDVS. I interviewed many of the artists myself on air before or after concerts and usually photographed them at the station and in performance.

My first interview was with local favorite Greg Kihn. He was an easy interview and such a nice guy that I never thought twice about trying to grab an interview with my favorite artists coming through town: Devo, the Rubinoos, Ramones, Readymades, the Beat, Ultravox, Iggy Pop, The Police, 20/20, the Fast, Talking Heads, the Twinkeyz, John Cale, the Pop, and Wazmo Nariz! Heady times for a new music fan, and I've got some of the photos to prove it—unseen for forty years until now.

Flamin' Groovies. 1978. (L to R) Cyril Jordan, George Alexander. Rio Theatre, Rodeo, CA

Flamin' Groovies. 1978. (L to R) Chris Wilson, Mike Wilhelm. Rio Theatre, Rodeo, CA

The Knack. 4/12/80. The Recreation Hall at UC Davis, Davis, CA

The Knack. 4/12/80. The Recreation Hall at UC Davis, Davis, CA

The Knack. 4/12/80. The Recreation Hall at UC Davis, Davis, CA

The Pop. 1979. Slick Willy's, Sacramento, CA

The Beat. 1979. UC Davis Quad, Davis, CA

The Beat. 1979. UC Davis Quad, Davis, CA

The Beat. 1979. (L to R) Larry Whitman, Paul Collins. KDVS-FM at UC Davis, Davis, CA

The Rubinoos. 1979. KDVS-FM at UC Davis, Davis, CA

20/20. 10/26/79. KDVS-FM at UC Davis, Davis, CA

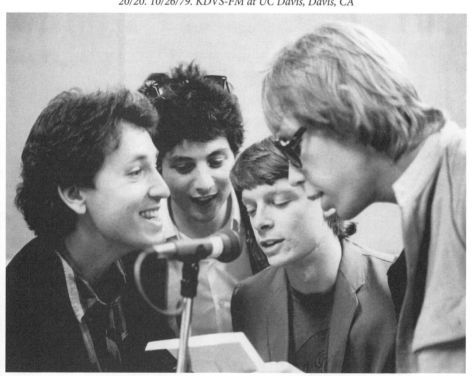

20/20. 10/26/79. KDVS-FM at UC Davis, Davis, CA

20/20. 10/26/79. ASUCD Coffee House at UC Davis, Davis, CA

Redd Kross. 4/5/87. Moby Disc Records, Sherman Oaks, CA

Ramones. 10/26/79. (L to R) Dee Dee Ramone, Joey Ramone. KDVS-FM at UC Davis, Davis, CA

Ramones. 10/26/79. KDVS-FM at UC Davis, Davis, CA

Tom Gracyk *has been a Record Store Guy in the Los Angeles area for forty years, first at Moby Disc for twenty-two years and since then at Freakbeat Records in Sherman Oaks. He has worked at times as a music writer, disc jockey, and photographer in the pursuit of free records, CDs, and concert tickets.*

Pag: The Bilingual Power Pop Pioneer Who Became Québec's First Rock Star

By Thierry Côté

ASK MUSIC FANS FOR a definition of "power pop" or a list of who classifies as a power pop act and who does not and you are likely to get dozens of different, ambiguous, and often contradictory answers. Sure, there are some elements that are found in many quintessential examples of power pop songs: ringing power chords, Beatles- or Beach Boys–influenced harmonies, an almost maniacal reverence for the hook, and lyrics about romantic—often adolescent—yearning. However, once you get past those sonic or lyrical touchstones, debates about who and what fits the tag are commonplace, something that is rendered easier by the fact that even some of the most prominent names associated with power pop (Cheap Trick, Todd Rundgren, Flamin' Groovies) have spent much of their careers dipping in and out of the genre. The year 1972 is often acknowledged as the birth of American power pop, marked as it was by the releases of both Big Star's *#1 Record* and Todd Rundgren's *Something/Anything?* as well as by Raspberries reaching the top five of the pop charts with the epochal "Go All the Way." Anyone paying attention to the sounds coming from north of the border, though, may have noticed that a young, long-haired French Canadian with dark, piercing eyes was not only already mining similar territory, but also finding significant commercial success with that music, setting the stage for Canada to be a fertile ground for power pop for decades to come.

Born in the Ahuntsic neighborhood of Montréal in November of 1948, Michel Pagliaro—"Pag" to his fans—became obsessed with his father's Cuban big-band records and doo-wop music at a young age and already owned his first guitar by the time he turned eleven. Soon, Pagliaro was part of the first wave of Québec rock & roll bands, making his Montréal club debut as a fifteen-year-old and playing in several groups (Les Stringmen, Les Bluebirds, Les Merseys) before joining Les Chanceliers in the summer of 1966. Initially recruited as a guitarist, Pagliaro quickly established himself as the charismatic lead vocalist and frontman of Les Chanceliers. Like most of the new groups bursting onto Québec's music scene in the mid-1960s, Les Chanceliers took their cues from both the yé-yé movement in France and the British Invasion, releasing covers and adaptations of recent French and Anglophone chart hits: the Beatles' "Drive My Car" became "Tu peux t'en aller," James & Bobby Purify's "I'm Your Puppet" became Pagliaro and the group's first hit, "Le p'tit popy," the Rascals' "How Can I Be Sure" turned into the moody "À Paris la nuit," and so on. While the A-sides were usually polished, polite covers, the flips of these early 45s often featured Pagliaro originals that hinted at a burgeoning songwriting talent—"La génération d'aujourd'hui" in particular, with its crashing drums and a searing guitar solo, is an excellent garage-rock youth anthem worthy of a spot on any Nuggets or Pebbles compilation.

In 1968, Pagliaro left Les Chanceliers to embark on a solo career that was immediately successful thanks to a pair of songs originally recorded by French pop superstar Claude François:

"Comme d'habitude" (later adapted in English by Paul Anka as "My Way"), which reached number two and spent sixteen weeks in the Québec charts in 1968, and "Avec la tête, avec le cœur," a 1969 chart-topper. He also hit number one with the original composition "Pour toi pour toi," which earned him a BMI Certificate of Honor for his contributions to Canadian music, but not much in terms of rock credibility. Again, as successful as Pagliaro was at this time, he seemed more destined to become Québec's answer to Glen Campbell or Engelbert Humperdinck (whose "Wichita Lineman" and "Call on Me" he also adapted in French) than Québec's first true rock star.

This all changed with a trip to London in 1969, where Pagliaro spent time recording and reworking his image. He returned to Québec in the fall with longer locks, a look influenced by mod fashion, and a batch of new, harder-edged songs that better fit his new Jim Morrison–like appearance. The first of these to be released as a single in 1970, the blistering "J'ai marché pour une nation," revealed a new Pagliaro, one who wrote his own material with his musicians instead of adapting existing hits, a rock singer with a huge, heavy sound closer to Cream and Deep Purple. His evolution continued with "Give Us One More Chance," his first English-language single with national distribution for the Much record label. An elegant ballad with hints of Procol Harum's "A Whiter Shade of Pale," "Give Us One More Chance" also boasts one of Pag's most soulful vocals. While writing in English certainly opened up new markets, Pagliaro did not view it as a career move but rather an attempt to "try new things."[1] "Give Us One More Chance" also showed beyond the shadow of a doubt that a francophone singer from Montréal could produce credible, world-class rock music in English. As Pagliaro's introduction

---

1 Ian McGilis, "Paglophiles take heart," *The Gazette* (Montréal), Jan. 20, 2000.

to the anglophone audience, it was a resounding success: the song made Canada's top ten in 1970 and earned him another BMI Certificate of Honor. But Pagliaro was just starting to hit his groove.

Next up for Pagliaro was the first of three quintessentially power pop singles he released over the span of a year that could all conceivably be described as the best Badfinger song Badfinger never recorded. "Lovin' You Ain't Easy," released in 1971, is simply two minutes and forty-three seconds of pure power pop ear candy, a song blessed with crisp production, arena-sized power chords, shimmering acoustic guitars, an instantly unforgettable melody, angelic harmonies, and more hooks over its brief running time than most full-lengths. Recorded at Apple Studio in London (whether in part or in its entirety remains unclear), "Lovin' You Ain't Easy" displays both a sophisticated arrangement and an effortless musicality that could have made it a worthy candidate for inclusion on an early Paul McCartney solo album had it been penned by the ex-Beatle (down to the melodic bassline and the subtle "woo-hoo" in the outro), but with the extra oomph that made songs like Raspberries' "Go All the Way" or "Let's Pretend" burst out of speakers. It was a huge hit across Canada, selling more than 50,000 copies and reaching the top ten in English Canada while hitting number two in Québec, where it spent an astonishing thirty-seven weeks in the singles charts. In the United States, it drew the attention of *Cash Box*, who noted its "McCartney-ish touches" in its December 25, 1971, issue as well as its "potential to spread across the border,"[2] but the single ultimately tanked there.

Not that Pagliaro cared: "M'Lady," released a few weeks after "Lovin' You Ain't Easy," was already well on its way to the top of the

---

2   "Choice Programming," *Cash Box*, December 25, 1971, 94.

Québec charts, where it would stay for four weeks. Just as catchy as "Lovin' You Ain't Easy," "M'Lady" is a more muscular brand of power pop, sounding not unlike Janis Ian's "Society's Child" as performed by George Harrison's *All Things Must Pass* orchestra on amphetamines. That its chiming electric and acoustic guitars (including a particularly Harrison-like slide part) and lively wall-of-sound production would recall the late Beatle's magnum opus is perhaps no coincidence, as word circulated in late 1970 that Pagliaro had met Harrison during a visit in London earlier that year and that the two had already begun working together.[3] Though the rumor remains unconfirmed, it is not inconceivable that Pagliaro, already recording at Apple Studio, could have dropped in on a Harrison or Badfinger recording session. In any event, "M'Lady" continued Pagliaro's winning chart streak and confirms that while not usually included as one of the originators of power pop alongside Badfinger, Raspberries, or Big Star, he was certainly dipping his toes in the same waters.

Finally, "Some Sing, Some Dance" confirmed that "Lovin' You Ain't Easy" and "M'Lady" were no flukes and that Pagliaro had a real knack for meticulously crafted, hypermelodic three-minute perfect pop gems. On the unabashedly romantic "Some Sing, Some Dance," electric guitars mostly take a backseat to brightly strummed acoustics in a spacious, airy mix that features more Beatlesque harmonies, a prominent string arrangement and even castanets. Recorded at Toronto Sound Studios, where Rush would soon put its first album to tape, it is perhaps Pagliaro's most impeccable studio creation—and was another hit across Canada. No less an authority on power pop than Greg Shaw wrote in *CREEM* that "Some Sing, Some Dance" was "so

---

3   "Michel Pagliaro et George Harrison des Beatles travailleront ensemble," *Télé-radiomonde*, November 28, 1970, 29.

charming I can't restrain myself from playing it at least ten times a day,"[4] and in *Phonograph Record Magazine* likened the recording to "the *Revolver* Beatles with Phil Spector at the controls."[5] Once again, *Cash Box* predicted a US hit in pop markets for this "all around interesting song with a great arrangement that really deserves several listenings,"[6] but despite getting some airplay in US stations, American chart success wasn't in the cards for Pag. Nevertheless, "Some Sing, Some Dance" belatedly received the stamp of approval of another power pop pioneer as Emitt Rhodes joined Ray Paul on a 2000 cover of the song that marked the former's first new recording in twenty-seven years.

Pagliaro never really revisited the kind of power pop that he perfected over the span of these three songs and that led Alan Betrock to list him alongside Raspberries, Big Star, Curt Boetcher, Stories, and Sparks as one of the North American exponents of a "pop revival" in 1973.[7] Instead, Pag turned his attention to a more primal and elemental brand of rock 'n' roll best exemplified by raw, fiery adaptations of "Riot in Cell Block No. 9" ("Émeute dans la prison"), "Walking the Dog" ("Faire le trottoir"), and "Lucille," as well as originals like "Louise" or "J'entends frapper" that earned him the praises of American critic Richard Meltzer ("Everything Monsieur Pagliaro touches seems to be a full realization of some

4   Greg Shaw, "Juke Box Jury," *CREEM*, January 1973, 78.

5   Greg Shaw, "*M'Lady/Pagliaro/Pag/Pagliaro Live*," *Phonograph Record Magazine*, 1973, [accessed July 28, 2020] https://www-rocksbackpages-com.ezproxy.library.yorku.ca/Library/Article/michel-pagliaro-m146ladypagliaropagpagliaro-live.

6   "Choice Programming," *Cash Box*, September 9, 1972, 16.

7   Alan Betrock, "The Sweet: *The Sweet*," *Phonograph Record Magazine*, September 1973, [accessed July 28, 2020] https://www-rocksbackpages-com.ezproxy.library.yorku.ca/Library/Article/the-sweet-the-sweet.

rock and roll idea"[8]). There were also more detours, as Cajun ("Ti-Bidon"), country ("T'es pas tout seul à soir"), Texas boogie (the autobiographical "C'est comme ça que ça roule dans l'nord"), reggae ("Cinéma") influences showed up in Pagliaro's music, and 1981's minimalist *Bamboo (Cuisine Kung Fu)* suggested that he had payed attention to new wave.

While he remained wildly successful in Canada—and especially in Québec—well into the 1980s, becoming the first Canadian artist to earn a gold record in both official languages and continuing to reach the upper echelons of the pop charts with his singles, success in the United States and abroad eluded him. In fact, his career outside of Canada tells a classic power pop story: lots of excitement in some corners of the music press, but very little to show for in terms of record sales or chart placements. Some of the blame for this can certainly be traced back to unsupportive record labels that repeatedly shelved single and LP releases—none of his albums ever made it to the United States. But Pagliaro himself admitted that he was not really willing to make the necessary concessions or to sacrifice his other projects just to achieve success down south. After years of failed attempts at achieving wider recognition in the United States, Pagliaro conceded that his desire to be his own boss probably did not make things easier: "I come up with my own finished product; it's the only way I can work."[9]

Michel Pagliaro has continued to perform live and tour on a relatively regular basis since his last studio album in 1988 (I saw him perform in 2016—his first Toronto concert in many decades—and his voice showed no sign of age), but for fans

---

8   Richard Meltzer, "Quebec's music scene: Rock trails, time warps, and total alienation," *The Gazette* (Montréal), Jul. 3, 1976.

9   Juan Rodriguez, "Pagliaro has his own $300,000 studio," *The Gazette* (Montréal), Dec. 16, 1978.

anticipating new music, the story has mostly been one of dashed hopes, missed deadlines, and repeated promises of forthcoming new songs that never quite materialize. Always interested in the technical side of music—not only an in-demand producer, he also moonlighted as a tape editor, learned to cut vinyl lacquers, and quickly built his own studio—Pag's perfectionism, which served him well on those pristine early 1970s power pop singles seemed to start to get the better of him by the end of the 1980s. After a decade-long wait and hints that a new album was almost complete, Brendan Kelly of *The Gazette* quipped, in 1997, "followers of this absurdly non-prolific fellow will, of course, believe it when we actually see the new studio album in stores."[10] By 2000, Pagliaro was becoming increasingly evasive and told Ian McGillis that the new album would be coming out "sometime this millennium."[11] In December 2005, Pagliaro sounded an optimistic note when he told *The Gazette*'s Juan Rodriguez—who got to hear nine tracks from sessions dating back to 1997—that the album would be out in 2006, once he finished laying down final vocal tracks: "It's coming."[12] And again in 2008: "It's coming, it's coming."[13] However, following three more years of studio silence, the singer sounded resigned while doing press for the 2011 reissue of his albums on CD, perhaps even defeated: "Maybe it'll be posthumous. Who knows?"[14] Perhaps Pagliaro was not being facetious when, asked

---

10   Brendan Kelly, "Bran Van 3000 set to ink international deal," *The Gazette* (Montréal), Nov. 3, 1997.

11   Ian McGilis, "Paglophiles take heart."

12   Juan Rodriguez, "What the hell he got?," *The Gazette* (Montréal), Dec. 11, 2005.

13   Juan Rodriguez, "On Pagliaro," *The Gazette* (Montréal), Apr. 26, 2008.

14   Brendan Kelly, "Iconic rocker Pagliaro finally changes his tune," *The Gazette* (Montréal), Dec. 8, 2011.

at twenty-three about his plans for the future, he mused, "Never settle down, never stop writing. Then when you're fifty, you're out of the game. Retired."[15]

Will we ever again hear new music from Michel Pagliaro? As the years go by, even Pag himself no longer seems sure of it. If and when we do, it is unlikely to sound anything like the trio of power pop singles that helped make him a revered figure among fans and music critics both in Canada and abroad—and that's fine. In the early 1970s, Pagliaro went into the studio looking for a sound, a blend of rousing open chords, shimmering acoustic guitars, and soaring melodies; once he found it, his restless creative spirit pushed him and his music in new directions. But those songs, those three beautiful, masterful singles—they're still as good as power pop can be.

---

15   Iain MacLeod, "Pop artist seeking big break in U.K.," *The Calgary Herald*, Feb. 10, 1972.

Thierry Côté *is a writer, music critic, and adjunct professor of Political Science and Communications at York University in Toronto, Canada. He has studied the intersection of popular music and international relations as well as the treatment of musicians as threats to national security. He would always rather be listening to music or playing tennis—ideally, both at the same time."*

My Fantastic Place

By Chip Jacobs

C HRIS DIFFORD AND GLENN Tilbrook: your music is my joy machine. Now cough up $500.

Here's why. On college party nights my junior year, friends would cram into my stucco apartment for our peculiar brand of artistic appreciation. Once properly red-eyed, we'd pick our favorite song, assume a handstand, and then allow pals to hoist us up to the ceiling to "moonwalk" upside down. Dirty heels were imprinted to quality rock—the Police, U2, Cheap Trick—being blared. I, however, only inverted myself for *you*. Squeeze was the sound I'd been waiting for from the black hole left by John Lennon's murder and the shallow onslaught of hair-metal. When "In Quintessence" hit that record needle, I went up.

Speedy guitar paired with mordant lyrics about a blowhard adolescent with a pretend girlfriend ignited something in me.

He smokes himself into double vision
Leaves his mind on indecision
Thinks he's invented imagination
Says that God is some relation

You know who didn't have any imagination? My landlord, who at semester's end eyeballed ceiling tiles mucked like a mosh pit and declared that I wouldn't be getting back my security deposit. So, thank you for that.

And bless you for everything else.

For forty-odd years, Squeeze has remained one those mystifying talents whose exceptional catalog many American pop connoisseurs overlook. Like the Kinks before them, their hunger to experiment in the studio, which they considered their sonic laboratory, made them elusive to pigeonhole. They were also frequently the right band at the wrong time.

Think about them as a *National Geographic* special might. Squeeze's dominant characteristic would be Chris and Glenn singing in octave-apart voices that magically harmonize into something both knowing *and* infectious. Its natural habitat: the pebbly streets and sandy roads of England from which they mined "kitchen-sink dramas" that make you laugh, tear, or simply marvel at how they pulled it off. Its growl: Telecaster-fueled arrangements that know when to blaze and when to recede. Zoological superpower? Easy. The ability to produce a lightness of being in those who encircle it.

I was in the crowd at an Orange County amphitheater to see them after graduation in 1985, knowing that their precocious success had thrust them so close to the sun that they'd had to reconstitute after dissolving. I cared little, hearing music pulsing with new wave synthesizers, nods to Elvis, rockabilly beats, and guitar hooks that'd have Jimmy Page a smidge green. Squeeze's oft-sardonic lyrics about romance were just as profound as its music was versatile, too. When they crooned "if I didn't love you I'd hate you," I grinned, because that's how I felt about the mercurial girlfriend next to me.

Listening that night after seeing so many performers who filled setlists with libidinous and macho themes that told you zero about the human condition was a reminder of the brawn of pithy, tactile descriptions. In the elegiac "Vanity Fair," there's the dropout who "paints her nails on the bathroom scales." In the giddy "Piccadilly," you smell the yellow curry en route to fireplace nooky. In fan favorite "Up the Junction," you wince for the man who lost everything after "the devil came and took [him] from bar to street to bookie." In "Revue," you howl as they skewer a nose-picking, D-list TV host in his "dickie bow ties."

◆◆◆

THE BEST POP SONGWRITING duo of their era, guys you may foggily remember from radio hits like "Black Coffee in Bed" or their wacky MTV videos discovered each other through Chris's magnificent lie. With fifty pence he swiped from his mother's purse, he posted an ad in a London shop window. Wanted: guitarist "into" the Beatles, Small Faces, Glenn Miller, and others "for [a] band with record deal and touring." When a younger teen in pink trousers and no shoes turned up, he learned that there was neither an established group nor sealed contract. But why quibble when you're a match introduced to kindling?

Chris, nineteen, was jet-black haired and shy behind his cockiness, a once chubby kid with dyslexia, imaginary friends, a knack for poetry, and a gypsy's prediction he'd discover happiness through music. After reading a Pete Townshend interview about the rock-star life, he decided the gypsy was right. Glenn, with his long nose and slight lisp, was a more extroverted persona and the organic musician between them. He'd been booted out of school for refusing to shear his hippy-long blond locks. Chris first noticed him sitting in a flower bed playing guitar like a "beardless Jesus."

The working-class boys united by musical sensibilities and older brothers with health problems penned 137 songs in a flashflood of creativity in 1973 and 1974; they frequently wrote in all-nighters thick with candles, weed, and ambition. As the pop-rock world slobbered over *Goodbye Yellow Brick Road* and *Band on the Run*, the duo was chiseling their future. A future where they'd sell out Madison Square Garden, earn a Grammy nomination, appear on *Late Night with David Letterman*, and license their music for film and commercials. A tomorrow where they'd become an English heritage act, the subject of a *BBC* documentary, and count Elton John, Paul McCartney, and Johnny Depp as enthusiasts.

Two became one in their songwriting ritual. Chris would scribble lyrics on notepaper, sometimes without lifting pen from pad, and leave them for Glenn. He'd vanish for days or weeks, and then slip his much fussed-over arrangements on a cassette under the door for his partner's delighted ears. Miles Copeland, their first manager, realized they could be huge.

They performed originals and covers, playing for beer money. They saw contemporaries in Dire Straits and regarded the Sex Pistols as annoying. Rounding out their lineup was now the effervescent Jools Holland on piano and keyboard, the resourceful Gilson Lavis on drums, and the first of several bass players. John Cale, formerly of the Velvet Underground, produced their maiden album by pressuring them to lean into punk rock. While they untucked shirts and affixed safety pins for him, it was an unnatural fit for pop-rock troubadours who tilted new wave. Boom! In "Take Me I'm Yours," a marching, synchro-beat propels a traveler journeying across the desert toward belly dancers on a tired camel. Deejays and younger audiences thirsted for more.

Their first US tour wasn't exactly screaming girls and popping flashbulbs, just the same. At their first gig, they jammed before an audience of a man and a dog. By the second set, the dog was gone.

Oh, well: they traveled in a van, gelling and growing, with Lavis doing his wild-man Keith Moon impression. Their second album, *Cool for Cats,* reflected musical growth hormone. In "Goodbye Girl," the repeating keyboard mimics the quixotic heart of a man who awakens from a one-night stand with a woman who robbed him blind. While Glenn was the Squeeze's front man on vocals and guitar, Chris, who played rhythm, sang the title song in a cockney rasp. Seamlessly, he goes from cowboys and Indians to his own life as a local celebrity who fraternizes with villains and groupies, the latter of whom gave him "a nasty little rash."

Argybargy, their follow-up, better defined them in the music-verse as more eclectic than the Cure and less abstract than Depeche Mode. There were rockers like "Pulling Mussels (From a Shell)," which explodes out of the chute, and "Another Nail in My Heart" with a footfalls riff and a silky lead. Deeper in was "Vicky Verky," a bubble-gum-fast ditty exploring forbidden love and abortion, and the boogie-woogie of "Funny How It Goes" about hitting on "champagne women."

Then drumroll. The record that *Rolling Stone* touted as one of the best albums of the decade, the record I wore into vinyl exhaustion, was 1981's *East Side Story.* Here, Squeeze smashed its mics through the walls frowning on pop rock risk-taking. It throbbed with blustery youth ("In Quintessence") and hummable, blue-eyed seduction ("Tempted"); it had female depression ("Woman's World") about a housewife so unfulfilled by "shiny appliances" that she can barely stagger home from the pub. The sleeper is the tear-jerking country ballad "Labelled with Love," told with the care of a novel in which the protagonist reflects back. In this case, it's an arthritic widow returning to her native England from the Texas prairie amid the ruins of alcoholism.

She unscrews the top off from her new whiskey bottle
Shuffles about in her candle-lit hovel
Like some kind of witch with blue fingers and mittens
She smells like the cat and the neighbors she sickens

Produced by Elvis Costello, *East Side Story* was a revelation, a comet streaking across the top-forty sky. But then something awful happened. Music critics and their record label dubbed Difford and Tilbrook "the next Lennon and McCartney." This was some rarefied stuff, the first time the "B" word was credibly invoked in the post-Beatles vacuum. Squeeze painted urban scenes and quirky people with uncommon dexterity, and the unified sound of Glenn and Chris singing together is eerily similar to John and Paul doing it, especially in their pre-*Revolver* days.

Yet where the Fab Four went from mop-tops to pathbreakers exploring war, psychedelia, and the British Establishment, Chris depicted inner demons, absolution, and, much later, in "Please Be Upstanding," erectile dysfunction. Sure, Glenn's voice resembled Paul's in pitch and ability to modulate, but his musicianship was as much influenced by *his* idols, Jerry Garcia and Jimi Hendrix, as George Harrison's.

The world craved the next Beatles, however it got it. The music industry, meanwhile, needed a new darling even though Squeeze's disdain of typical song patterns and fuzz-box crutches made them a more boutique act on the margins of the genre than power pop torchbearers like ELO and the Cars.

Inside the group, the buzzy comparison was as much millstone by flattery. On cue, egos bloated, coke vials filled, and, as Chris admitted, band members started rowing in different directions. Dizzy by the parallels, fried by the tour-record-tour-record drudgery, Squeeze still sallied forth. Even their spotty albums contained notables. "King George's Street" is a marital split, expressed in power chords and emotion, through the eyes of children. In the brassy "Hourglass," they bagged their biggest US hit. "Melody Hotel," a twangy takeout about a family man who abused prostitutes, would've been an ordinary group's encore sensation.

Before splitting up again as fissures widened between creative, stubborn Glenn and fragile Chris, who'd previously bailed on a US tour, self-medicating with vodka, powder, and isolation, Squeeze's tenth album sparkled. It just gleamed in 1993 as grunge rock overtook the airwaves. In the blazing "Third Rail," the narrator gives the bottle choking him its walking papers. "It's Over" is an acoustic-guitar wall of sound about corrosive jealousy.

Transcending them all was "Some Fantastic Place," the name of the record and arguably the song at the top of their mountain. It pays tribute to Glenn's ex-girlfriend, the one there at Squeeze's inception, as she lay dying of leukemia while describing the afterlife where she expected to be headed. The chords reverberate like "My Sweet Lord" and the lead is divine, all culminating in a church-like hymnal that parts the clouds of mortality. When my mother died in 2008, I cried myself into spiritual peace listening to it.

> *She showed me how to raise a smile*
> *Out of a bed of gloom*
> *And in her garden sanctuary*
> *A life began to bloom*

◆◆◆

IT'S 2012 AT THE Greek Theater, and Squeeze has reformed after close to eight years in which Glenn and Chris were no longer on speaking terms like a married couple at wit's end. An energetic audience swayed and lip-synched to their classics and clapped for muscular new tunes. When the curtain dropped to make way for the headliner, the B-52s, I seethed. The band that gave us "Rock Lobster" would be blessed to have written any of Squeeze's B-side treasures—"The Truth," "The Elephant Ride," "Slightly Drunk." How, I grumbled, could Donovan and the Beastie Boys be in the Rock and Roll Hall of Fame yet not them?

No Squeeze. No justice.

Two years later, I milled outside a small club waiting for Glenn's solo show. When he climbed out of his bus, I zipped up to clasp my hero's palm. After a crisp set, I reapproached him for an autograph, nervous as a schoolgirl. I babbled that I wanted to steal "Labelled with Love" for a short story, and the man who brought me so much pleasure flashed angry eyes at me. I tried digging out to say I wished it inspired a play, not realizing it had—in 1981. Glenn smiled, chuckling like an older sibling who saw what this moment meant.

At that point, I was upside down again on my old college ceiling, delirious, $500 forgotten.

Chip Jacobs *is a bestselling author and journalist whose books include the historical novel* Arroyo, *the social critque* Smogtown: The Lung Burning History of Pollution in Los Angeles, *and the biography* Strange As It Seems: the Impossible Life of Gordon Zahler. *A multi-award-winning writer (and eternal Beatlemaniac), Jacobs' reporting has appeared in the* Los Angeles Times, The New York Times, CNN, Los Angeles Daily News, Pasadena Star News, *and elsewhere.*

Blow You Away

By Brian Vander Ark

L ISTEN FOR THE HARMONY," Mom would whisper to me before she and Dad rose from the church pew, shuffling to the altar to sing the musical sermon at Sunday services. "That's my part." Dad wore Buddy Holly glasses and sang the melody, the man's role, while Mom, her hair held high by the chemicals in Aqua Net, made the ladies proud.

Pre-divorce, secular music was not allowed in the house unless it was the vanilla sounds of the Ray Conniff Singers. Their version of "Dueling Banjos," called "Dueling Voices," was on repeat, me listening over and over to learn all of the lady parts. When the ban on popular music was lifted from our house, I looked for secular harmonies and found the Archies and the Partridge Family.

By the early eighties, I'd built up too much of a tolerance for bubblegum pop; the hangover from "The Things We Do For Love" wasn't worth the high. Naturally, I took the gateway and dipped my toes into power pop. I craved harmonies with heavy guitars, a chaser for the bombast of bass and drums. It was hard to find what I was looking for in Grand Rapids, Michigan, where my classmates only devoured what MTV fed them.

I felt I'd missed all the good stuff growing up in that pseudo-conservative town when I joined my first band, His Boy Elroy. We were a punk cover band, a description that should have begotten a more fitting name like the Oxymorons. Bad monikers aside, being in a band parted the mainstream; I found a group of power pop lovers who introduced me to Utopia, the Plimsouls, and XTC.

XTC was an immediate favorite. The jingle-jangle guitars, the gratifying harmonies. Guitar solos that were honest-to-goodness parts. The energy that overflowed on *Drums and Wires* spilled into *Black Sea*. *English Settlement* sounded like the Beatles had gotten back together for another *White Album*. *Skylarking* was a greatest hits album of songs not yet released. On *Live in Concert 1980,* Dave Gregory and Andy Partridge play the meticulously crafted, stern, steady guitar notes with joyful abandon, Colin Moulding's bass and Terry Chambers' drums offering a sturdy safety net. With a rowdy crowd of riotous footballers in his palm, Partridge sings those early XTC songs with such bravado that it's hard to believe he suffered a nervous breakdown shortly after.

◆◆◆

WHEN I FORMED THE VERVE Pipe in 1992, I wanted to write lyrics like Partridge's. To bully the English language a bit, tease it for its flaws. I wanted to write songs with guitar parts that sounded as if they were built on a fragile foundation of sand; one strong wind blows a note out of place, and the whole goddamn thing falls apart. I wasn't interested in the concrete support of strumming three chords.

So, I channeled the power pop muse, opened my kaleidoscope eyes to the sky, and asked for some gifts; songs that critics would one day call my power pop gems. But the muse was nowhere to be found, and I broke the cardinal rule of power pop, writing an undeniable big, fat, goddamn American hit single. And not one fucking harmony on the track.

The song, "The Freshmen," is a cautionary tale of two college boys who did some things they will regret one day. Tap, tap, tap on my shoulder. Like writing a hit song and not being able to follow it up with another, perhaps?

That's where my mind was during those three weeks at the number-one spot on the Billboard Alternative charts. As Mom said, "That's my part." Okay, listen, write hits, forget all the harmony shit. Don't be a one-hit wonder, your career will end with the follow-up single mucking around at the bottom of the Billboard chart, up to number seventy-three, down to number ninety-nine, back up to number ninety-five for a week of teasing and nowhere to be found the next. So, no harmonies, and if you'd like some sweetener with that, double the lead vocal in the chorus. That'll give you your fix!

I gave up listening. Didn't listen to the music I loved, didn't listen to my bandmates' suggestions, didn't listen to my instincts. I listened instead to the voice that told me I was born to write hits. I'd already broken the seal. From here on out, I needed to write hits like the ones my contemporaries wrote, bands I didn't even like. I judged every single on the radio. Damn, this song needs a bridge, how could it be top ten? We still need bridges, don't we? Are we giving up on bridges?

Andy Partridge saved me. I got a call from EMI Publishing. Knowing I was a rabid XTC fan, they suggested I go to England for a writing session. Andy was working on a new XTC album and interested in cowriting. Holy shit.

I assumed Andy wanted to write a big, fat, goddamn American hit too, with real heart-on-your-sleeve stuff. I was going to be a cowriter on the first number #1 XTC song in America. Of course I was! It was only two years ago that Andy had visited the us in the studio during the recording of the last Verve Pipe album, produced by his old friend Jerry Harrison. Popping his head in at Jerry's request, Andy listened to a few songs, looked directly at me and said, "I'll have to look out for you." Satellites orbited my ballooned noggin after that compliment.

◆◆◆

A WOMAN DIED ON my flight to England, an omen good or bad. If nothing else, it was a great story to break the ice with Andy.

Swindon was the Grand Rapids of England, houses lined in neat rows under overcast skies, suburbs with charming cottages forgotten by Her Majesty, inhabitants left alone like good little self-sufficient subjects. Andy met me at the door, amiable, a cup of tea in his hand. I stepped into the house and immediately thought of my parents. It was pleasant, smelled of antiques, old books, chimney ashes. I could hear the Kinks coming from the living room. "I'm really into them lately," he said, perhaps hopeful that we would have a discussion. I had very little knowledge of the Kinks, not enough to talk below the surface of their hits, so I thought this was the best time to nervously blurt out, "A lady died on our plane."

"Oh, my," he said. "I'll bet that's a great story."

Turns out it wasn't. She died. You gave away the ending, idiot.

"Let me just get that tea for you." He returned and found me delighted to see our latest album on his CD player, the case open. Andy gave it a nod. "I listened to it this morning, but I was unable to make it past...song...three," he said, those three drawn-out words signaling his disapproval. Okay, he called it "that" record and not "your" record, so shift the blame to the label, bandmates, mixer. I did, and he saved me with, "You know an album that is mixed impeccably?" Oh, shit, he's going to name some obscure band from the late sixties. "This one," he said, holding up Aerosmith's *Pump*.

There's hope for me yet.

◆◆◆

ANDY SHOWED ME AROUND the place, all of it erased from memory when we entered the room of a thousand soldiers. They were miniature, meticulously standing at attention, shoulder to shoulder, filling every shelf on every wall in the room, top to bottom. "Holy shite," I squeaked out, and immediately regretted not using the good old informal American "holy shit."

We walked the path through the back garden to the shed, his musical tool shop. It was filled with equipment, some old, some new, some obsolete; wires everywhere, like out of an eighties sci-fi movie. He had set up two amps to face each other, a microphone between them, to be turned toward whoever had a song idea worthy of amplification.

I plugged in the guitar he loaned me, pulled the notebook out of my new Union Jack backpack. Goddamn it, I tried too hard. Once settled in, he reached for the DAT recorder and hit record. "All right, Mr. Bonker, bonk your bonk," he said as he started up the drum machine.

Of the two days spent there, we filled a DAT tape with a dozen ideas, good and bad. The best, and the only one that would eventually see the light of day, was "Blow You Away." It was a marvelous mix of T. Rex and Raspberries, Bowie and Badfinger. He sang nonsense lyrics, gibberish over a guitar riff, a few feet from my face. I was in a pop bubble with the master.

The night before my flight back to the states, Andy took me to a local restaurant where we ate curry and drank pilsner. He encouraged me to ask him, just ask him, anything and everything I wanted to about XTC, as long as I didn't share too much of it. I asked and got my answers. The artificial crackling at the end of "Sacrificial Bonfire"? I know what it is. "Another Satellite"? I know what (who) it's about.

After dinner, we returned to the shed where Andy sat me down behind his little mixing board, turned the lights low, and opened a folder on his computer labeled "Apple Venus Demos." "Would you like to have a listen?"

I let out a little sob. It had been years since I'd listened for pleasure.

◆◆◆

I WROTE THE VERSES for "Blow You Away" on the plane the next morning. (I'm happy to report no one died on that flight.)

Teasing me forever, kiss me and then never come up for air
Why don't you blow, blow, blow, blow
Shiver at the sight of beast and beauty
Standing upright in a hurricane
Why don't you blow, blow, blow them all away?
And start again.

It was XTC with a touch of the Verve Pipe; sexy, suggestive, a hint of bubblegum at its saccharine center. I loved it. With a shot of power pop in my arm, I thought it was safe to take our new album in this direction. We'll even call the album *The Verve Pipe*, eponymous as if this is who we really are. Radiohead had one hit and survived going their own way and we can too.

The band recorded "Blow You Away" and sent it off to EMI, who submitted it for the soundtrack of what would certainly be an enormous hit movie, *The Avengers*. We went into the studio and recorded an album that intended to bridge the gap between American rock and roll and the British Invasion, full of heavy guitars and harmonies. An album that might even do as well overseas as our albums do here in the states. I'll be an international sensation.

The movie and our album were a one-two punch, but neither landed. The single never had a chance, never even made it on our record.

I've spoken to Andy a few times over the years, pleasantries mostly. I regret never thanking him for reigniting my pleasure for listening, but that load-bearing weight belongs on my shoulders. I've realized my purpose; I'm a soldier among thousands, standing at attention, yet seeking existential answers, looking for the perfect lyric, listening to generals and majors of the genre I love, all as it should be; from a distance.

After all, my part is listening.

Michigan native **Brian Vander Ark** *is the lead singer and songwriter for the multi-platinum rock band the Verve Pipe, recognized worldwide for their smash hit "The Freshmen." On his own, Brian maintains a multifaceted career not only as a musician, having released four acclaimed independent solo albums, but also as an actor, featured motivational speaker, and writer, with the upcoming release of his autobiography* When I Was Young I Knew Everything.

Hold My Life

By Jim Lindberg

THE FIRST TIME I HEARD the Replacements song "Hold My Life" was during college in San Diego. I lived alone in a tiny studio apartment off Fifty-Sixth Street in off-campus housing with students who were either too cool or too old for the dorms, drunkenly partying until all hours of the night. There were rows of two-story apartment buildings on either side of the street on a sloping hill, usually shaped like a horseshoe around an infrequently cleaned pool. I didn't have many friends there, so most of the time I was catastrophically lonely. I couldn't help thinking I existed in some kind of purgatory between two lives, even while surrounded by 20,000 faculty and students.

I bought the cassette tape of the Replacements album, *Tim*, one Saturday morning at a Blockbuster down the road from school. This was my idea of big weekend fun back then, perusing the bins of record stores for hours on end, looking for hidden gold, hoping that no annoying coed sales associate would appear over my shoulder to ask if they could help me find something. *"Oh, yeah, sure. Could you just search my mind for all my secret hopes and dreams—my innermost desires and aspirations, my triumphs and defeats, my lost loves and silent yearnings—and suggest a perfectly empathetic seven-inch single that would go along with my plight in life? Maybe the soundtrack to a Jonathan Demme film? No? Well, then fuck off and let me shop in peace!"*

I'd spend hours in the store looking around, not because I enjoyed it that much, but because it was really all I had to do other than go back to my wood-paneled apartment, make a bean and cheese burrito, and feel sorry for myself. I'd read something in the school paper about a band called the Replacements and thought it was such a great name that they had to be good. (Although I found the album cover art to be particularly hideous and nearly put it back on that account alone.)

I remember struggling with the impenetrable shrink-wrap in the parking lot, yanking the cassette out of its plastic cage and popping it into the tape player. A few brief seconds of anticipation passed as the tiny pinwheels began to rotate and the delicate, thin, brown silicon reel-to-reel tape threaded itself into my crappy Radio Shack stereo. Then the first song came roaring through my speakers, all raging distorted guitars and ill-timed drums. *"Well, well, well, I...."* the music and scratchy-voiced vocals filled the corners of my car with its cracked, imitation-leather upholstery. I have to be honest, I had no idea what the singer was saying for the first few lines. I just bobbed my head along with the disjointed tempo, my internal rhythm detector silently approving of the propulsive, swaggering gait and loose, lo-fi production—but then it came to the chorus and the words hit me right in the chest: *"Hold my life...until I'm...ready to use it."* I stopped the car in the middle of the road and stared at the tape player while the song played on. I immediately knew one thing for sure—this song was mine. It was written for no one but me and my fucked-up existence at school. I felt completely out of step with everyone around me, like a lost dog separated from his pack. Thank God a random bastard in Minnesota felt the same way I did because for some reason this made it all okay.

The song was like salve on a burn. It made the pain of loneliness feel good somehow, made it noble. Screw all the smiling, cocky frat boys and giggling sorority girls having such a great time outside my window, drinking and carrying on at all hours of the night while I sat alone in my apartment unable to sleep from all the noise. They didn't know pain. They didn't know loneliness. They also didn't know that the Replacements were the best band in the world and the fact that they played sloppy and out of tune just made them that much better. They all listened to Wang Chung and the Outfield and shitty pop radio bullshit. Me and Paul Westerberg were tortured souls. We were drunken poets. We drank cheap red wine and rot-gut whiskey and quoted Baudelaire from the rooftops. They'd never understand.

♦♦♦

WHETHER YOU JUST LIKE the Replacements or you *really fucking love* the Replacements kind of depends on whether you're a Rolling Stones or Beatles fan. Yes, technically we're all both, but if you had to pick a desert-island album—*Rubber Soul* or *Let It Bleed*—which one would you choose? The Beatles practically wrote the Bible on popular rock music; their wide-ranging stylistic output and evolution from "She Loves You" to "Helter Skelter" to "Let It Be" makes Elvis Presley's musical kingship seem a lot less royal. Their matching suits, moppy haircuts, and bubblegum sweetness inspired legions of screaming, eardrum-shattering fangirls. The Stones, on the other hand, with their wasted, rough-side-of-town swagger, provided a more dangerous, devilish antidote to all that pomp and pop. You listened to "Michelle My Belle" and "Yesterday" on commercial AM radio in the seventies, but *Some*

Girls was an album made expressly for FM stereo on your dad's giant speakers. Listening to the stuttering, phased-out sound of a song like "Shattered" made you feel like you were doing something dirty. If the Beatles were *Playboy* magazine, the Stones were *Hustler* and *Cheri*—a lot smuttier and more scandalous. Both were revolutionary, but only one could get you sent to confessional.

The Replacements loved both, but were firmly rooted in the Stones tradition. The guitars sounded out of tune, the drummer didn't really sound like he cared if he was keeping time or not, and the singer mumbled so much you didn't know what he was saying in the verses all the time, but it didn't matter. You knew it was something sarcastic and cool.

In my opinion, good power pop is "Saturday Night" by the Bay City Rollers, "What I Like About You" by the Romantics, and "My Sharona" by the Knack (definitely all in the Beatles tradition). Great power pop is "Hold My Life" by the Replacements, "Bittersweet" by the Hoodoo Gurus, and "Surrender" by Cheap Trick (in the Rolling Stones tradition). You can hear Keith Richards' loose, whiskey-fingered guitar chording all over the Replacements songs, tracks where you could practically smell the cigarette smoke in the reel-to-reel tape. Power pop as a genre came about because the bands were difficult to classify (Urge Overkill and Pegboy didn't sound all that punk, but they sure as hell weren't pop). Bands who had the danger and shambolic delivery of the Stones were destined to be my soul mates. We could never play as good as the Beatles, could never write a song like "Norwegian Wood," and it's likely at some point we might be brought up on drug charges.

So I listened to *Tim* from start to finish while staring at my cassette player, drinking in song after hooky song. "Bastards of Young," "Waitress in the Sky," "Left of the Dial," "A Little Mascara"—each one hitting every screwed-up, out-of-tune note perfectly; each lyric bending a different heartstring, a symphony for the out of luck, out of step, and out of time. Until, at last, came "Here Comes A Regular." What the fuck is this? A song about drinking in some shitty dive bar where it's so dark you can't see anything except the little Christmas lights dangling sadly from the overhang above the barstools, relic from some soggy holiday years ago? But then your eyes adjust and you see small groups of people scattered around, secretly slouching in booths, old guys sitting slumped over the bar (some alone, some in pairs), and the bartender is grumpy and cleaning glasses in the sink. They all turn and squint when you open the bar door and let in the forbidden sun, reminding them there still is a world outside. Then they see it's you and they all yell out your name so loud it's like you've come home from a long foreign war, when in fact you were just there yesterday. It's a song about drinking buddies feeling glorious and shitty in the same breath. You both stare into the golden richness of the frothy beer in your glass, complaining about how fucked the world is, but at the same time so perfectly wonderful in its raggedness, with so much heartache, and misery, and pain, and joy that the two of you should probably just punch each other in the face right now as hard as you can; then have a shot of something dark, hard, and strong, and laugh and cry and let out all the frustration and pain you've ever felt in your whole life, the shame and embarrassment and sheer joy of being human and alive, at the wood-paneled, blinking neon bars in any small town from here to anywhere.

Are you kidding me? Who is this Paul Westerberg? *Who are these Replacements?* I must join them, and we will drink cheap beer and take shots of Maker's Mark and scream ourselves raw until the sun comes up peeking through the houses as we stagger home through the rain-wet streets. And we'll sleep on each other's couches and make macaroni and cheese out of an old pot for breakfast, and then Bob will make a joke about how *"it's always happy hour somewhere!"* before pulling the tab on a Schlitz. We'll laugh and say he's crazy, "It's not even noon yet! We can't possibly start drinking again this early." Bob's having none of it; he throws me a freezing cold can of Pabst Blue Ribbon that hits me square in the chest and it hurts like hell, but I don't care. I crack the beer and take a pull and it tastes really good, like it's washing the hangover and the sins of the world right off of me. Then Tommy says…well, you probably already know what Tommy says.

That's why this music spoke to me on that Saturday, all alone in my shitty Datsun 210 with the leaky radiator. I sat there alone with the engine idling in front of Blockbuster, drumming along in time on the dashboard, smiling in resigned recognition. It told me that I was a Replacement, that I wasn't friendless and alone as much as the world tried to convince me otherwise; that I had friends who thought exactly like I did and we would take on the world together. The rest be damned.

Jim Lindberg *is the lead singer and songwriter for veteran Hermosa Beach based skate punk band Pennywise and the author of the book* Punk Rock Dad. *He's also the subject of the Showtime documentary* The Other F Word, *cofounder of Action Sports and Music Network HavocTV, and a Punk Rock Literary website, PunkGuru.com.*

Greetings from Pop Music City, USA

By Bill DeMain

B EING A POP MUSICIAN in Nashville in the 1990s was like being
Rodney Dangerfield. You could have a big local following,
with all your artistic ducks in a row, but I tell ya, you still couldn't
get any respect. At least not outside the city limits.

New York and LA looked down their bicoastal noses at our
pop music. Their A&R people would come to our festivals like
Summer Lights and Monsters of Pop, and then loiter in the back
of the room, talking over the music. If they liked something, they
might make an overture to an artist, but inevitably say, "It's good,
but I'm not sure there's a market for it…"

Subtext: You're from Nashville.

The world beyond America didn't even know we had pop
music. The thinking went, Nashville is a country town. It's the
Grand Ole Opry, rhinestones, and fringe. It's Hank and Johnny
and Loretta and Garth. Despite the fact that country artists like
the Everly Brothers, Roger Miller, and Dolly Parton had crossed
over to the pop charts many times successfully, the perception
remained that there couldn't be a credible pop scene in Nashville.

I admit, I wasn't convinced either when I moved here in 1988.
But there was and there is pop music. And with a bit of selfish pride,
I'll say that I was part of an amazing scene in the mid-1990s through

early 2000s that I believe finally changed people's perceptions about Nashville. That scene included Bill Lloyd; the Shazam; David Mead; Fleming & John; Ross Rice; Fluid Ounces; Self; Amy Rigby; Joe, Marc's Brother; King Bub; Josh Rouse; Sixpence None the Richer; Daniel Tashian; Who Hit John; Swag; Pat Sansone; Millard Powers; Luxury Liners; Kim's Fable; Evinrudes; Lifeboy; These Are Houseplants; Will Kimbrough; Venus Hum; Brother Henry; Will Owsley; Lambchop; Doug Powell; and my own duo, Swan Dive.

That list is in no particular order, but I did put Bill Lloyd's name first because he was the senior member of our crew, a trailblazer with two seminal albums under his belt, *Feeling the Elephant* and *Set to Pop*. Bill moved to Nashville from Bowling Green in 1982. There wasn't much of a pop scene then, but he pushed things forward in early bands the Bullets and Practical Stylists. He wrote songs for MTM Publishing, where he met Radney Foster. Together, they formed a duo that scored several top ten country hits in the late eighties. Songs like "Sure Thing" and "Hard To Say No" smuggled Byrds and Beatles style cargo into commercial country radio. But by the mid-nineties, Lloyd had swung most of his attentions back to pop, and was often referred to as the "godfather" of our scene.

"There was a really high quality of songwriting going on during that whole period," Lloyd tells me. "Not all of the bands had the crash-bang-boom of traditional power pop, but this being Nashville, a songwriter's town, the level of craft was consistently great. Power pop can be its own ghetto, with a lot of extraneous elements—the right polka-dot shirt, the right haircut, songs only about girls. So in some ways, the scene in Nashville, being song-driven, became more diverse and interesting."

So how to describe the diverse music we were making anyway? Well, it was pop. It was powerful. It had all the elements you want and need in pop music—romantic longing, good grooves, smarts, hooks, and harmonies galore. So, yes, it was power pop, in the broadest definition. Add to that the underdog status we all felt, and collectively, you had a movement that was bristling with energy, creativity, and I'll-show-you attitude.

And as corny as it sounds, it felt like family. Just like the Opry. The Grand Ole Popry.

At the center of it all was one of Nashville's most influential figures, Brad Jones. Multi-instrumentalist, artist, songwriter, producer, arranger, studio owner, and force for good, Jones has an incredible résumé. He played bass with Matthew Sweet, Marshall Crenshaw, and Ron Sexsmith. He made an underground classic solo album, 1995's *Gilt Flake*. And at Nashville's unofficial pop headquarters, Alex the Great Studio (which he co-owns with Robin Eaton), he's produced or mixed eighty percent of the artists I mentioned above, as well as Jill Sobule, Imperial Drag, Butterfly Boucher, and Chuck Prophet (he also produced Cotton Mather's *Kontiki*, a power pop landmark). When I listen back to all that music, Swan Dive's included, I'm struck by how fresh and original it sounds. Though Jones has fully digested all the main power pop sources—Beatles, Beach Boys, Byrds, Big Star—his interests are far more Catholic, taking in glam, rockabilly, bossa nova, soft rock, hard rock, blues, girl group, soundtracks, jazz, and yes, even country. Because of his large palette, his pop productions have unexpected textures and flavors. One of the first things Brad ever said to me, during a Swan Dive session, was, "I'm a parts guy." And he was right. The parts that he added always elevated a song above what you might expect in a surprising, even subversive way. A pedal steel would come swooping in over a minor ninth chord. A banjo or sitar would enliven a solo spot where you'd expect a guitar. The belly of a Basset Hound would provide a hands-on percussion part that gently drives a track.

It was always in the name of making memorable pop music.

"I love the architecture of the three-and-a-half minutes in a pop song, the order of events," Jones tells me. "As a producer, I don't start thinking about anything else—how loud the drums should be, what guitar will be best—until we figure out the architecture. Tearing the song apart, figuring out what's stronger (the verse or the chorus), getting rid of the chorus and making the bridge the chorus—I try to convince the artist to try some pretty radical things sometimes. But all in the name of making the parts flow together. It's a cumulative effect. Something should always be blooming, roiling, heightening, and deepening in the architecture. The songs we all love do this. Think of 'Baby Blue' by Badfinger, and how the third verse feels. When you get there, somehow it's built to that, in lyrics, in melody. There are the right amount of measures, the right amount of textures. It's alchemy, and sometimes it's hit or miss. You have to try this or try that until you get the lucky combination."

It was definitely a lucky combination that made Swan Dive the first of the pop acts to break out beyond Nashville. And it was all thanks to Jones. In the fall of '96, he was touring Japan with Marshall Crenshaw. He brought along a few copies of our first self-released record, which he'd produced, and gave them to people he met along the way. "Hey, check this band out." One fell into the hands of a prominent journalist. She wrote a gushing review in a magazine. A lot of people read it. Within a month, I was getting calls at home in Nashville from A&R execs at EMI, Pioneer, and Sony. At first, I thought, "Yeah, right, Japan. It's one of my friends playing a prank." But it wasn't.

Then I got a call from a guy in Tokyo named Yoshi Nagato. He had heard our record, loved it, and asked if he could act on our behalf to get us the best deal. After checking out his credentials, I realized that he was one of the most-respected people in Japan's music business—a Dick Clark type who had worked in every capacity, from record store owner to A&R to artist management.

Sony licensed our first record, repackaged and remastered it, had us shoot a video, then brought us to Japan for a promotional tour. It would be the first of five trips from 1997–2004. Those visits were like stepping into a parallel universe for me and my singing partner Molly Felder, a place where we were loved for simply being us. A place where the lost values of pop music were still celebrated. We hadn't changed anything about our sound or how we dressed or acted, but whatever it was about Swan Dive that had been continually falling through the cracks in the US, in Japan it was perceived differently. No one at the label ever said anything to us about format or how "there wasn't a market for it." They loved our music, got behind it, and released it. And the Japanese listeners embraced it. I can't tell you how surreal it was when I saw our first single climbing up the charts, right next to Janet Jackson, George Michael, and REM. It was equally surreal the first time Molly and I went into Tower Records in Tokyo—this is the mothership Tower, eight stories high—and were greeted by the one-two-three punch of our record playing in-store, our video on twenty TV screens, end-display listening stations with our cardboard likenesses, and our CD right next to Paul McCartney's latest, *Flaming Pie*.

There was also a weird nostalgic overtone that worked in our favor. We found out that the biggest-selling western pop act ever in Japan was the Carpenters. Bigger than the Beatles, Elvis Presley, or Michael Jackson. I also found out that the Japanese adore happy-sad things—what the Brazilians call saudade, the combination of love and longing laced with melancholy. They love French cinema like *The Umbrellas of Cherbourg* and *Amélie*. They love *One Hundred Years of Solitude* by Gabriel García Márquez. They love Bossa Nova. And they love the Carpenters, the duo whose music is essentially the sound of heartbreak wrapped in a pretty major seventh chord.

Which was Swan Dive's sound too.

In one of the first interviews we did, a journalist said, "We think that you two are like the new Carpenters." We heard it many more times over the years. No, we weren't siblings. But yes, we were a guy-girl duo. And Molly played drums and sang in a voice not unlike Karen's, a pure, beautiful sound with a shiver of rainy day hurt. I like to think that our success in Japan had to do with the merits of our music. But there may have been some Carpenters nostalgia nudging it along.

One more thing. When people talk about power pop, the Carpenters aren't usually mentioned alongside the Beatles or the Beach Boys (though they covered "Ticket to Ride" and "Fun, Fun, Fun"), or any of the mostly male bands. That seems unfair. They may not have had power chords or big beats, but Richard and Karen had tunes to die for (some they wrote, some heavyweights like Burt Bacharach and Hal David or Roger Nichols and Paul Williams wrote), walls of harmonies, and that happy-sad feeling that's at the heart of everything from the Beatles "If I Fell" to Matthew Sweet's "I've Been Waiting" to Jellyfish's "That Is Why."

After Swan Dive broke though, many others from the scene did too.

But let me pause for a moment to acknowledge a few other folks who were instrumental in nurturing pop in Nashville. The late journalist Jim Ridley was a true-blue fan and promoted all of us in our city's weekly, *Nashville Scene*. Keith Coes at Radio Lightning was a champion and gave airplay to all of us. Lee Swartz and Jason Wilkins organized and promoted festivals and events. And Mike Grimes, a musician himself, opened Grimey's Records and the Basement club, both forums for all of us.

Okay, back to the artists. David Mead got signed to RCA in New York, toured with Fountains of Wayne (Adam Schlesinger produced David's excellent second album *Mine and Yours*), and has had songs in TV shows like *Ed* and *Private Practice*. The Shazam played sold-out shows in the UK, recorded at Abbey Road, and has worked with producer Mack (ELO, Queen). Joe Pisapia from Joe, Marc's Brother toured with alt-popsters Guster for years, then went on to produce k.d. lang and Ben Folds. Millard Powers has been playing bass with Counting Crows for years. Amy Rigby has written an acclaimed autobiography, *Girl To City*, and tours with her husband, Wreckless Eric. Bill Lloyd toured as a utility guy with Cheap Trick and wrote songs with them, as well as for Marshall Crenshaw and Marti Jones. The Evinrudes signed with Mercury. Sixpence None the Richer signed with Reprise and had a worldwide hit, "Kiss Me." Their singer Leigh Nash has had a successful solo career, working with producers Pierre Marchand and Brendan Benson. Pat Sansone has been a multi-instrumentalist member of Wilco for years and has his own acclaimed band the Autumn Defense. John Painter of Fleming & John, an in-demand string and horn arranger, has worked with Ben Folds, Kelly Clarkson, and Brandi Carlile. Daniel Tashian's group the Silver Seas had great success in the UK and songs in shows like *Breaking Bad*. And in 2019, Tashian won an Album of the Year Grammy for producing and cowriting Kacey Musgrave's *Golden Hour*.

"Just the fact that pop music can invade a record that's a CMA favorite like Kacey Musgraves tells you a lot about how the scene in Nashville has changed," Brad Jones says. "Daniel and Ian [Fitchuck, his production partner] could sneak those more advanced melodic and harmonic elements into what other people think of as just a country record, and that's fantastic. And there've been so many cool rock and pop bands that have come up in the last ten years. Quichenight, Jetpack, the Carter Administration. And Tristen and Caitlin Rose are both wonderful pop artists now. It's a great time to be making nontraditional pop and rock in Nashville. Everything is wide open now. All the styles are all intermingled. Just the fact that there are hip-hop beats in country hits tells you something. People aren't fussy about their definitions anymore, which is liberating."

To Brad's list, I'd add Nicole Atkins, Los Colognes, Rayland Baxter, Andrew Combs, Gabe Dixon, Emily West, Larkin Poe, and the Secret Sisters. I could go on. Suffice it to say, the pop scene is alive and well. Rodney Dangerfield no more.

But for me, and I think many in our late nineties scene, the defining moment came in 2011. Taylor Swift, on her way to becoming the biggest pop star on earth, was in the middle of a hometown sold-out show at our Bridgestone Arena, and played an impromptu version of "Nashville," a great song written by David Mead ("Maybe I'm a fast train rolling down the mountain..."). It may have been lost on most of the 20,000 adolescent fans there, but when word got out, it buzzed around amongst our Popry family on social media. And I thought, "We won. We moved the needle. We changed things. We showed the world that Nashville was more than a country town."

Bill DeMain *has released ten acclaimed albums (plus two solo records). He's written songs for and with many artists, including Marshall Crenshaw, A Girl Called Eddy, Curtis Stigers, Teddy Thompson & Kelly Jones, and David Mead. Bill's also a BBC correspondent, a noted journalist who's contributed to* Mojo *and* Classic Rock, *and the owner of Walkin' Nashville music history tours.*

Out of Time: The Material Issue Story

By Balin Schneider

UNLIKE MANY OF THEIR 1990 Chicago counterparts, Material Issue's unique sound was a combination of power pop and punk. Their energetic live shows, fronted by lead singer, guitarist, and songwriter Jim Ellison, made them one of the bands to watch in the Chicagoland area. While they did briefly burn on the national stage, their ascent to the major leagues of the music business was suddenly and tragically cut short by Ellison's suicide on June 20, 1996. His death put an end to the band. The sad truth is that they were both ahead of their time and before their time, and simply too power pop for their moment in rock. Plus, Ellison was a ticking time bomb, and they simply ran out of time before it all blew up.

In 2018, I interviewed the surviving band members, Ted Ansani (bass) and Mike Zelenko (drums), as well as music critics, managers, family members, famous musicians, and fans for a film on the band and its legacy. *Out of Time: The Material Issue Story* examines the legacy of Jim Ellison on power pop following his untimely death. Over the two-year period that I conducted these interviews and worked on the film, I came to understand the tragedy of a group that came close to, but never achieved, superstardom. The title of my film comes from something legendary Chicago rock critic Jim DeRogatis told me, "They were out of time for their entire freaking career. They were mods twenty years later. They were pioneering alternative pop makers four or five years too early."

I first heard of Material Issue in 2016, when I was sixteen years old, scouring the internet for old punk bands. I was hypnotized and drawn to their debut album, *International Pop Overthrow*, perhaps because every song on the album sounds like a single. My dad said this is what had drawn him to the Who in his day—the sharp melodies and cacophonous din of the drums and guitars. When my girlfriend picked up the Material Issue CD for me, it inspired me to do some research on the band. It was then that I learned about the tragic story of Ellison's suicide. A couple of months later, I decided that I had to tell Jim, Ted, and Mike's story.

When I first explored what made the band unique, I was constantly drawn back to that first album, a captivating set of demos that had been recorded for fewer than $5,000. A true power pop veteran, Jeff Murphy of Shoes, had produced the sessions that resulted in their debut single, "Renee Remains the Same" backed with "The Girl Who Never Ever Falls In Love." After extensive, high-rotation airplay on Chicago's excellent rock station, WXRT, "Renee" put Material Issue on the map in the city of big shoulders.

But just as important as a local hit single, it was the strong work ethic of the band, and Ellison in particular, that propelled them to the next level. Jim was not just the band's front man and songwriter, but right from the start he'd also been their booking agent and manager, working tirelessly to get them every possible club gig going. Prior to working with Mike and Ted, he had played and recorded with Danny Thompson (currently of the band Face to Face) and Lance Tawzer (currently of Thrift Store

Halo, previously in the Lupins), who told me that Ellison "was the most driven person I've ever met."

Following the success of the "Renee" single, Material Issue played hundreds of shows at prominent Chicago venues like the Thirsty Whale, the Cubby Bear, Metro, the Vic Theater, and the Avalon Ballroom, where they sold copies of the single and EP directly from the merch table. In true post-punk DIY fashion, Ellison, Ansani, and Zelenko had sat in Jim's bedroom in west suburban Addison putting "Big Block Records" labels on their self-pressed records. Jim was also a big advocate for the music community in Chicago—he lived it, he loved it, and he made it all happen, frequently inviting up-and-coming bands to open for Material Issue at big venues, pulling them along as the band forged ahead into the mainstream.

Additionally, Material Issue's independent spirit became an inspirational model for other Chicago bands like Smashing Pumpkins, Urge Overkill, Liz Phair, and Veruca Salt on how to make it without a "proper" record label.

After saving up their own band money to record the demos with Murphy, the indie album *International Pop Overthrow* was picked up by a major label, Mercury Records, in 1991. Mercury's Bob Skoro had brought them to the label, and after he and other executives went to Chicago, a number of major national record labels likewise flooded into the city looking for the next big act, finding among them the aforementioned Phair and Smashing Pumpkins. It's important to note, however, that Material Issue was the *first* band of that era to put Chicago on the map as a center for the power pop renaissance.

In 1991, the band signed a management deal with Jeff Kwatinetz and Peter Katsis to handle their affairs, and despite never having managed a band before, the team would soon go on to work for an eclectic roster of some of the biggest acts in music, including Jennifer Lopez, the Backstreet Boys, Audioslave, and Ministry.

International Pop Overthrow got the band onto MTV, with videos for "Valerie Loves Me," "Very First Lie," and "Diane," which was played in heavy rotation and on *MTV Spring Break* in 1991. MTV veejays Matt Pinfield and Dave Kendall were huge proponents of the band, booking them on MTV's *120 Minutes*. Jeff Kwatinetz later told me that as the band continued to tour extensively behind the debut album, he had set up a deal with the label to release the band's cover of "Mrs. Robinson," to be included in the remake of *The Graduate*. But when Mercury would not fund the video, the gig ended up going to the Lemonheads instead.

When the band finally got off the road, they regrouped in the studio with Jeff Murphy to make their sophomore album, *Destination Universe*, which featured even more great songs, including "What Girls Want," "Everything," and "Next Big Thing." In 2002, "Everything" would finally see some radio success when an acoustic cover by Dallas, Texas, band Stereo Fuse became a most-requested song in the South and Midwest US. It even became a top-ten music video and entered the Billboard top twenty in 2003. But back in 1992, such success would elude *Destination Universe*, which failed to capitalize on the staggeringly successful 300,000 copies sold of *International Pop Overthrow*. Jay O'Rourke, the band's friend and unofficial fourth member, couldn't understand the sophomore jinx, particularly after being blown away by the single "What Girls Want."

"I heard the song," O'Rourke told me, years later, "and I was like, I'll never see these guys again. I thought the song was going to be huge, I mean, like huge, and to this day, I don't know why it wasn't."

Seemingly undaunted, however, the band soldiered on, maintaining a loyal and intense fan base by playing on huge tours opening for INXS and the Pretenders, and even headlining their own tour of Europe. Everything seemed to be pointing upward for the band, especially after they hired Blondie producer Mike Chapman to record their third album, *Freak City Soundtrack*, released in 1994. During the sessions, the band brought in some heavy friends, including Illinois rock royalty Rick Nielsen from Cheap Trick and Chip Z'Nuff from Enuff Z'Nuff, plus Pat DiNizio from the Smithereens, and even Gilby Clarke from Guns 'N Roses. While Ellison wrote more than enough songs for the album, including the stellar "Going through Your Purse," "I Could Use You," and "She's Goin' through My Head," they even managed to squeeze in their first ever cover, the Green Pajamas song "Kim the Waitress." Years later, Mike Chapman told me that Jim thought the single reminded him of Debbie Harry finding the single on Blondie's cover of the Nerves' "Hanging on the Telephone." "Kim the Waitress" was chosen as the band's first and only single off *Freak City Soundtrack*. I consider this album to be a stellar work of musicianship from the band; it still astonishes me that it didn't break higher. It just didn't sell what it needed to, and the band stalled. Then Mercury dropped them.

While they seemed lost, they nevertheless got to work on new demos and tried to find a new identity and enjoyed a camaraderie with pals like Phair and Urge Overkill. Ellison and Zelenko even joined the Wild Bunch, a supergroup of sorts with Clarke, DiNizio, Z'Nuff, and Blondie drummer Clem Burke, sponsored in part by Camel Cigarettes. Material Issue even recorded a string of covers with Liz Phair, one of which was, ironically, Blondie's "Hanging on the Telephone," which will be released for the first time ever in my film. Toward the end, Jim was trying to start a new band, perhaps with Zelenko, called AMX (American Music Explosion), but he couldn't get it off the ground. Ansani, Zelenko, Kwatinetz, Katsis, and the band's assistant and friend Melissa Zukerman urged Ellison to go to Los Angeles to write songs for other people, and a songwriting session was even set up there with Marshall Crenshaw. Ellison had just written "Rocket Boy" with Liz Phair for the film *Stealing Beauty*. According to *Chicago Tribune* music critic Greg Kot, many labels were eyeing Material Issue at the time. However, Ellison inevitably succumbed to his personal demons, compounded by the band's problems, and took his own life in his garage. After his death, perhaps the notorious Chicago-based producer and Big Black founder Steve Albini summed it up best: "He felt like he hit a home run, and nobody cheered."

Ellison's suicide, like all suicides, was the fateful result of a deeply complex set of circumstances. Material Issue's quick rise, followed by Ellison's even quicker fall, left Mike and Ted behind, but he also left a sister, mother, and father—not to mention the thousands of fans—who are still spreading the love and compassion of Jim's songs. I'm grateful for people like Jeff Murphy, Mike Chapman, Matt Pinfield, and Joe Shanahan that continue to fight for Jim's legacy. While the promised International Pop Overthrow never fully happened, Jim's music continues to reach a global audience, and even touched stars like Courtney Love, who covered "Valerie Loves Me" in shows with Hole, and Pete Townshend, who dedicated a song to Jim at the Who's Halloween show in Chicago in 1996. Jim and Material Issue are truly the shining example of a band that absolutely knew power pop— and did not care if they were surrounded in a world of grunge. Over time, their music continued to resonate within the Chicago sound with bands like Alkaline Trio, Fall Out Boy, Local H,

Naked Raygun, and Urge Overkill carrying on the band's power pop legacy. Ellison created a model for other bands from Chicago to make it, to thrive, and to get signed to a major label. Ellison loved his city and the music there. When Material Issue bottomed out, Jim Ellison lost his musical identity, and without that, he had nothing. Perhaps that was what broke him in the end.

There's something sadly prophetic in Jim's lyrics for "Renee Remains the Same" that could almost read as foreshadowing his own downfall.

He was the one who was most likely to,
but he never got her through,
and they barely made it by.
But if we look at her family picture,
I'm sure we'll see a face
that looks a lot like now.
I always wanted to get her attention,
I only got rejection, anyhow.

Balin Schneider *is a filmmaker and artist from Topeka, Kansas. His first feature film* Out of Time: The Material Issue Story *chronicles the story of Chicago power-pop trio Material Issue and their legacy.*

Once the Teenagers Leave the Fanclub

By R. Clifton Spargo and Anne K. Ream

Brooklyn, New York, March 2019.

THE CROWD AT THE Music Hall of Williamsburg is—as is usually the case in this part of Brooklyn—studied in its hipness. There are women wearing button-down boyfriend shirts actually borrowed from a boyfriend, and more than a few men sporting skullcaps and Brooklyn beards. The occasional slip dress or black tattoo choker is in evidence which, depending on the age of the woman wearing it, may or may not be a self-conscious homage to grunge. Every third person seems to be sporting Converse Chucks. Though age can be a difficult thing to determine among this casually well-heeled and well-maintained crowd, forty- and fifty-something former cool kids clearly dominate. But there are plenty of millennials in the house, and even a few Gen Z-ers, sporting Nirvana tees too new looking to be vintage.

They've come together, this crowd of 600 or so, to see one of power pop's greatest still recording and touring acts: Teenage Fanclub. When founding singer-songwriters Norman Blake and Raymond McGinley take the stage (the band's third founding member, Gerard Love, having departed in 2018), what's striking about them is how un-striking they are. Sure, they've physically changed. The bright and horizontal striped shirts they sported in their nineties publicity photos have been replaced by ordinary blue button-downs and tees, and the long hair Blake and McGinley shook around on their *Saturday Night Live* debut is long gone. But even at the height of their fame, the band's stage affect was as strikingly low key as it is during their set in Brooklyn: *Don't pay too much attention to us. Just listen to the music.*

And the music is, as ever, worth the listen. Teenage Fanclub has been a musical force in the United Kingdom for over three decades, retaining a devout following across Europe, the United States, and Japan. They're a cult favorite of the used-to-be-big variety, having famously beaten out Nirvana's *Nevermind*—which dropped the same year as Teenage Fanclub's breakout *Bandwagonesque*—for *Spin*'s 1991 "Album of the Year." Nirvana front man Kurt Cobain once called Teenage Fanclub "the best band in the world."

Whatever heights they may have reached, and in our estimation those heights are considerable, Teenage Fanclub were never able to sustain their earliest commercial promise, especially here in the US. Perhaps this was predictable, given how difficult it was for good rock 'n' roll to chart in the US from the nineties on. The fact that Teenage Fanclub was categorized as power pop probably didn't help much either. Power pop has spawned an extraordinary body of music made by a long list of should-have-been-bigger artists, from Nick Lowe, Big Star, the Records, and Raspberries to Matthew Sweet, Material Issue, and Velvet Crush, to name just a few. Blending the radio-friendliness of chart-topping Beatles singles with the edgier guitars of that band's infinitely cooler, less-played recordings ("Hey Bulldog" and "Your Bird Can Sing" spring to mind), power pop should have something for everyone. But it's the hill far too many great bands have died on, at least when it comes to enduring, global appeal.

Norman Blake, for one, has always disliked the power pop label. In a 2019 interview for *Magnet*, he refused the tag categorically, saying, "There are a lot of people out there trying to write melodic songs with fuzzed-up guitar, and they don't have very good songs. That's why power pop isn't a great term, because it sorta lumps everyone in together, all the bad writers with the good ones." And then, to put a fine point on it: "It's a term I don't really recognize and fancy in our music."

Blake's not alone in this sentiment. A great many rockers with power pop creds have worried that the term carries too much baggage, evoking bubblegum sentiment, screaming teens, stupid adolescent lust, and often inane lyrics that remind listeners of how little of life the singer's actually seen. Of course, a great many rockers haven't name-checked both "teenagers" and "fanclubs" in their band name, or given their breakout album a title that nods to the joys of jumping on the commercial bandwagon, or packaged that same iconic record in a bright yellow and bubblegum pink pop-art inspired cover. Some of those trappings were no doubt meant to be tongue in cheek. In fact, Geffen Records, the American label Teenage Fanclub signed to after a bidding war, originally proposed an album cover designed by their art department. But Teenage Fanclub wasn't having it. "I had the idea to do the exact opposite and make the cheapest sleeve ever configured," Raymond McGinley told *The Guardian* in 2019. "I used a free-to-use Microsoft clipart image….And we ended up getting sued by Gene Simmons, who claimed to have trademarked bags of money. So I'm trying to produce the cheapest sleeve possible as some kind of comment on the music business and we end up getting sued by Gene Simmons. I said to our lawyer: 'Can we just tell him to fuck off?' He said no, so we gave him five hundred dollars and a credit." Clearly, no gesture of ironic modesty goes unpunished in the record industry. The entire incident puts a fine point on the band's troubled relation to the effervescent commercial ambitions of power pop.

Part of what makes Teenage Fanclub's sound so enduring is the way they repeatedly and insistently deviate from the strictures of power pop, even as they write songs with the harmonic intensity and roundedness that characterizes the most memorable music of the genre. The typical power pop song is Merseybeat tight, guitar driven, and largely absent of complicated arrangements. From the start, Teenage Fanclub has managed to have it both ways, adding a sometimes lush, often feedback-fuzzy jamming quality to tracks that would have otherwise been a bit too power pop perfect. The band went into the studio for the first time inspired by a Dinosaur Jr. show in Scotland and toured with Sonic Youth early in their career. The affinity for both bands shows.

If Teenage Fanclub's early output had a distinctly indie, sometimes grungy feel—unpolished exuberance with a pinch of West Coast psychedelia thrown in for good measure—they were also always working a retro sixties vibe. On *Bandwagonesque* they found a formula that locked in their sound. "There weren't many people at the time making melodic pop records that were kind of sloppy too," Norman Blake told *The Guardian* in a 2019 interview about the making of the album. "The vocals aren't brilliant, the playing's alright…it's not been tidied up like a lot of records are these days. It captures young people trying to find their feet."

Teenage Fanclub has always been an "album band" playing in a singles genre. With that in mind, take a listen to these five brilliant and very different Teenage Fanclub songs off the band's three best albums, *Bandwagonesque* (1991), *Grand Prix* (1995), and *Songs from Northern Britain* (1998). Put your headphones on.

"The Concept" (Bandwagonesque)

THE FIRST TIME YOU hear it, you swear you've heard it before. The opening track on *Bandwagonesque* is a Norman Blake gem that jolts you out of the past only to plunge you back in with appreciation for all you missed if you weren't around for power pop's first waves. The song starts out with a loud, proud, feedback-y shimmer announcing that Teenage Fanclub are hip to the ear-bending cool of fellow Glaswegians Jesus and Mary Chain, then shifts into a gorgeous minor-key melody that is so saccharine and dark that the longing inscribed on the song just has to be doomed. The stability of the guitar stroke is crystal-tuned Raspberries, perfectly paced. All the jangly guitars and smarting harmonies surge in a rush of feeling that's already somehow gone wrong.

He's singing about a girl and she's got opinions that don't match his—that in and of itself is a refreshing twist on the genre. She's more than just the object of power pop lust. She's someone with her own longing ache, with some feminist backbone, who digs the Status Quo and perhaps thinks his long hair means his band should be more metal. She's more into him than he's into her, which means he's going to hurt her and he's already sorry. This is heartbreak with a twist—his regrets get dashed, not his hopes.

Spend a few hours listening to the larger power pop canon and it can feel like one long story of heartbreaks (his) caused by rejection or elusiveness or unattainability (all her). But "The Concept" is one of the least self-involved power pop songs ever written, and the hurt he's singing about isn't his own. There's just an aching sincerity as he begs to be forgiven for a wrong that is never named: "I didn't want to hurt you, oh, yeah / I didn't want to hurt you, oh, yeah," over and over. We can feel him running out of words.

And just when you think you've heard the tightest power pop song ever written, it blows up at the two-minute mark and slides sideways into a jam that feels like cleaned-up Dinosaur Jr. infused with a splash of angry, frustrated acid rock. And then shortly past the three-minute mark, the band switches it up yet again, spinning into a slow, meditative riff that casts us far outside the power pop orb, nary a lyric in sight. It's a gorgeous piece of schizophrenic virtuosity, a band breaking up with their own song like the girl the singer never learned to love. All we get for the last three minutes of the "The Concept" is *oh-oh-oh*'s, interlaced with distorted metal guitars. It's sweet, sultry, regretful, fading away but not forgotten—the melody and sentiment like the structure of a song we're still clinging to.

"Sparky's Dream" (Grand Prix)

For all the lush ambivalence of *Bandwagonesque*'s retro avant-garde sound—is it an ode to Alex Chilton and Big Star? Is it grunge on the verge?—Teenage Fanclub's 1995 offering, *Grand Prix*, plays to the dead center of what anyone could have ever meant by the term power pop. "Sparky's Dream," the best song on that album in our estimation, was written by bandmember Gerard Love and given its painfully lame name by Norman Blake (which the band liked, Love told a fansite in 1995, "because it was kind of dumb"). It's a track that is as pristine as anything Teenage Fanclub ever wrote, a geek ode to lost love in which Gerard Love sings about a woman whose hold on him is one part dream, one part she's leaving and he's got to get her back. The most searching aspect of this heartbreaker, which is said to have been inspired by Love's fling with singer-songwriter Juliana Hatfield, is that he knows it's over and he's still falling for her. If she lived in space, he'd build a plane to get near her. Or he'd pray for a little *Star Trek*-inspired, intergalactic help: "Out of luck so beam me up / To hear her talking again."

The lyrics are a mess of astrology and sci-fi and timeless, poetical star-gazing. The song's sidereal plot gets confused like a bad map when he takes "a wrong direction from a shooting star," a line that is all sensibility and less than sensical. It's the beautiful nonsense of desperate feeling. But those three-part harmonies and chiming guitars sound so hopefully exuberant, so quintessentially power pop, that they make us believe he might still, with a bit of luck—say, a chart-topping single like this song deserved to be—get the girl.

"Ain't That Enough" (Songs from Northern Britain)

As the members of Teenage Fanclub became masters of their power pop craft in the mid-nineties, they learned to find meaning in the practical encounter with what was right in front of them. Nowhere is the band's penchant for seeing the glass half full more in evidence than on their gorgeous ninth record, *Songs from Northern Britain*, our personal favorite. The album's best-known track, "Ain't That Enough," is an ode to the countryside, and something more. In the mode of a timeless pastoral, sung to an urban audience that fails to see the mysteries everywhere around them, the song asks us to encounter the given world again, as if for the first time. "Here is the sunrise, ain't that enough? / True as a clear sky, ain't that enough?" In this song, nature serves as a stand-in for the taken-for-granted, everyday beauty of the places and people who are closest to us. With its gentle harmonies and sweetly jangling twelve-string Rickenbacker chords, "Ain't That Enough" is melody as mantra, a deeply moving and slightly wry take on the overused, new age-y directive to "just breathe."

"Guiding Star" (Bandwagonesque)

It's a tribute wrapped in a lullaby sung with minimalist affect, this lovely homage to the front man of the legendary power pop band Big Star. Of course, there are plenty of influences that Teenage Fanclub might pay tribute to. To be a master of contemporary power pop is to be a master appropriator, in thrall to a long list of handsomely harmonic bands. But Alex Chilton served as a breakthrough inspiration for Teenage Fanclub, and later also as a mentor and friend. The Big Star influence on Teenage Fanclub has been so often noted—rock critic Jim DeRogatis admiringly describes *Bandwagonesque* as a "classic of tasteful thievery"—that it might lead you to underestimate how ably and subtly Teenage Fanclub is revising their Chilton, making music inspired by him that is absolutely their own.

Maybe the best way to experience Gerard Love singing "Guiding Star" is to listen with the chiming vocals of Chilton's "Jesus Christ" playing in your head. There's the nod to Big Star's *#1 Record* as Love sings "you're my number one"; there's Love's shoutout to a Jesus Christ who comes "knocking at my door," which might be about Christ the man, but might also be about the Christmas carol–styled "Jesus Christ" sung by power pop deity Alex Chilton. Either way, the song concerns itself with that moment when our passions defeat us: "When everything you own is lost / And every friendship has its cost." "Our karma's come undone," Love sings, and then offers a kind of beatific plea to his inspiration. "Hey," he sings, as if reminding the person he's singing to (who is always also his listeners), "You're my guiding star." Love sings the chorus complete with airy, guiding-star sentiment just the one time, no shifting in the chords or guitar strum. And then, coming in just shy of three minutes, the song breaks up in a quiet guitar shimmer that is like a vision of Jesus with really cool hair and a halo that is indistinguishable from the sun.

"Neil Jung" (Grand Prix)

IF ALEX CHILTON INSPIRED many of Teenage Fanclub's more shimmering sounds, the legendary Canadian rock 'n' roller Neil Young is definitively a non-power pop influence on more than a few of the band's tracks. The more one listens for it, the more one can feel the subtle influence of the man who has been called the "grandfather of grunge," a musical movement Teenage Fanclub was sometimes associated with but never fully inside of. On "Neil Jung," another standout from *Grand Prix*, the band dispenses with subtlety and playfully tributes Young as though he were an influence of the psychoanalytically subconscious, Carl Jungian sort. In the cacophonous opening bars, the song invokes Young's "Like a Hurricane," one of the all-time great anti-love songs. This is a song about desire, romantic and professional, that is disastrously fulfilled. Written by Norman Blake, and purportedly about his former bandmate, Scottish rocker Duglas T. Stewart of BMX Bandits, it explores the perils of fame and notoriety, the damage done by depression, and the fallout from a doomed affair embarked on in the public eye. The harmonies are pitch perfect, the guitar work is melodic, and the overall sound is dense but also exuberant. It's a serious song that is a strangely buoyant: more emotional power, less light-as-air pop.

"Alcoholiday" as Coda (Bandwagonesque)

DESIRE, UNFULFILLED, PARTICULARLY OF the youthful variety, is a through line in power pop. The thing you want is the thing you can't have, which is exactly why it's the thing you want. Teenage Fanclub writes songs about unrealized desire that rival the best of them—"There are things I want to do but I don't know / If they will be with you"—but this is a band that finds new ways to live inside the unrealized dreams and hopes that drive so many great power pop songs. Not unlike Nick Lowe, another genius of the genre whose creative output is always evolving, Teenage Fanclub manages to feel youthful while exploring timeless themes of love, connection, regret, and loss. Even as power pop connoisseurs and practitioners, the band never felt all that teenaged. It's great power pop, sure, but it's music that at its best speaks to the eternal longings in all of us. Teenage Fanclub is just shrewd enough to understand that there's a world of things they want to say, and they're always finding someone new to say them to.

R. Clifton Spargo *is the author of the novel* Beautiful Fools, *award-winning short stories, and writings on music and culture in* Huffington Post, The Yale Review, Newcity, The Wall Street Journal, The Atlantic *online, and* The Cambridge Companion to Bob Dylan.

Anne K. Ream *is the author of* Lived Through This, *a critically praised narrative and photographic memoir of her multi-country journey spent listening to survivors of gender-based violence. The founder of The Voices and Faces Project, an award-winning storytelling project, Anne's writing has appeared in* The Washington Post, The New Republic, Los Angeles Times, The Cambridge Companion to Bob Dylan, *and numerous other publications. Anne is a frequent contributor to Newcity Chicago, where she writes about the intersection between music, gender, and social justice.*

68% Pure Imagination:
My Time in Baby Lemonade and Love

By Mike Randle

I N THE SUMMER OF 1992, I lived in a very "lived in" four bedroom townhouse in Santa Monica, just blocks from the beach. One of my roommates, Rusty Squeezebox, was a former bandmate from the eighties. We were both working on our own songs at the time, but on the weekends we'd sit and listen to Big Star's *Third*, the Beach Boys' *Pet Sounds*, Love's *Forever Changes*, or any of the other classic LPs on our turntable. We also found inspiration in newer bands like Sonic Youth, Dinosaur Jr., Nirvana, and Pixies. It felt like the right time to start a band again.

I'd worked at the legendary McCabe's Guitar Shop a few years earlier and caught Black Francis and Joey Santiago of Pixies playing as a duo one night. And I'd seen Robyn Hitchcock during his *Eye* tour, which was amazing since he's as good a storyteller as he is a songwriter and performer. All in all, the early nineties was ripe for melody-driven, guitar-heavy pop/rock bands. And if your songs had some substance to them? Even better.

Rusty and I often popped down to Nomads back then, a rock club on Pico Boulevard in West Los Angeles (former location of the Club 88 music venue that had been around since the sixties). The owner, Jennifer Kelton, wanted the bands to know they could hang there and unwind without going broke, presenting musicians with great drink discounts. It was inspiring to see so many bands play their own music. Rusty and I were also listening to the first Pink Floyd record quite a bit around this time, so when Rusty came up with Baby Lemonade as our band name, it stuck.

Not long after that, I recommended that Rusty call my friend David Green about playing drums in the band. He had moved out from Minneapolis a few years before and was working at Aron's Records in West Hollywood. David and I briefly played in a band together with me on bass. He'd answered an ad out of the recycler after the first drummer, Joey Peters, left the band to play with his pals in Cracker and then, later on, Grant Lee Buffalo. David was a great drummer who'd cut his teeth playing alongside Twin City bands like Husker Du, the Replacements, and Soul Asylum.

So, we had a drummer. Now all we needed was a bass player. Rusty and I were both working at an indie record store called Moby Disc Records in Santa Monica. One day, in walks a skinny punker with a Phil Oakey-looking haircut. He walks up to the counter with an arm full of Big Star, Love, the Clash, and Killing Joke records. Rusty jokingly asked if he played bass. He laughed and said he did, and that he was looking for a band. That dude was Henry Liu and that was how the original Baby Lemonade lineup came together.

◆◆◆

THE SUMMER OF NINETY-TWO was ours, and we immediately started to learn the six or seven songs Rusty and I had written. A few months later we got our first gig at the Coconut Teaszer in Hollywood, but we didn't announce it or invite anyone because we wanted to use the show as a live practice. The show went well and we felt good about it. Our friend, Jeff Davis, loved what we were doing and offered to manage the band. We took him up on the offer, letting him book shows so we could work on our music.

Jeff convinced us to make a six-song demo tape, so we went into our friend John Would's studio in Reseda. John also owned a tape duplication company so he made us a nice, professional-looking demo tape right before my birthday in November. (I still have one of those tapes!) Jeff used one to get us (what was being billed as) our debut show at Nomads, but not until the new year. He also encouraged us to keep a few on hand at all times, so I always had five tapes with me. "Opportunity," he said more than once, "doesn't always present itself, but when it does you always want to be ready." One such opportunity presented itself November 28, 1992.

It was a Saturday afternoon. About half an hour before my shift was over, an older, thin, white dude walked in dressed like something out of *Three's Company*. He'd driven up in a Trans Am and had a medallion around his neck, a Tom Selleck mustache, and a curly Mike Brady blond perm. Dude was straight out of 1974. He strolled around the record shop, all the while tossing CDs and LPs into a shopping basket. As he made his way to the counter I saw it was all Love and Arthur Lee LPs, CDs, or cassettes—everything we had in stock.

He told me he was Arthur Lee's booking agent and that he was down the street at the club called At My Place on Wilshire Blvd. He introduced himself to me at "Tom Sweeney of Kaleidoscope Productions" and said that if I gave him a discount he'd get me tickets to the show. I told him I was driving up to Santa Barbara that evening, but I did tell him about my band and how we were all huge Love fans and knew how to play some of the songs. I gave him a copy of our demo tape, thanked him for stopping by, and wished him and Arthur good luck.

Fast forward to the spring of 1994. Baby Lemonade received an invitation to play South by Southwest in Austin, Texas. That same week we were "discovered" by a French DJ at the Coconut Teaszer. He came to LA in search of a band to book for two weeks of shows in Tahiti. We said "yes!" and felt like we'd hit the jackpot. After playing to a packed house in Austin and getting our name out there, we returned home to Los Angeles feeling rejuvenated, with a new focus being on finding the right indie label to release our debut record.

It was around this time that our manager (whose phone number was on the back of the demo tape) got a call from Tom Sweeney asking if we wanted to open for Arthur at the Troubadour in late April (we couldn't say "yes!" fast enough). After the show, Arthur asked us to be his back-up band (his "Love," if you will). So we spent most of May '94 working on a Love set for the first show with Arthur on June 2 at Raji's, an underground rock club in Hollywood where all the coolest bands played.

Meanwhile, after a few more Baby Lemonade shows, Jeff got us a deal with Sympathy for the Record Industry, an *uber* cool record label out of Long Beach run by a Svengali-type character named Long Gone John. Sympathy released our debut, *The Wonderful EP*, which garnered good reviews in the US, UK, and Europe later that year. We were stoked to be on a label that had released music by Hole, Redd Kross, and Rocket from the Crypt, to name a few. The EP featured four originals by Rusty and me, as well as our version of "Windchimes/Wonderful," a Beach Boys deep cut from the *Smile* era.

◆◆◆

THE NEXT YEAR, WE flew to Spain with Arthur to play the Serie B Independent Music Festival with the Posies and White Flag.

(the Posies even let me play bass on their version of Big Star's "In The Street.") Then Sympathy for the Record Industry released our first full-length album, *68% Pure Imagination*. The album was blessed with positive reviews, as well as tons of support from the international music community. (Madrid-based Roto Records later released *68½% Pure Imagination*, which was the same record with two different songs swapped out.)

The first half of 1996 saw us play a lot of shows in Los Angeles, San Francisco, Orange County, and San Diego. On May 17, we flew with Arthur to Denmark for a two-week UK/European tour. By this time, bassist Henry Liu had left the band and was replaced by Dave Chapple, who'd played in a Hollywood power pop band called Boys Named Sue.

The tour was a total success. Arthur had brought along an old friend, David Fairweather, who hooked the band up with tour promoter/booker Gene Kraut. The tour ended on the thirty-first and David Fairweather and Arthur Lee flew back to Los Angeles. Baby Lemonade stayed behind and played a sold-out show in York, England, that was put together by our close friend, Michael Harrison, who had seen one of our early 1993 Love shows in Venice, California. We flew back to LA a week later and found out from David Fairweather that Arthur had been found guilty of firing a gun in the air and was being sentenced the next day. The judge threw the book at him, handing him a twelve-year sentence like it was all in a day's work. We wouldn't see him again for five years.

In '98 Baby Lemonade signed with New York's Big Deal, a record label that already worked with power pop royalty like Shonen Knife, Nick Heyward, and the Wondermints. That October, Big Deal released our second album, *Exploring Music*. Dave Chapple had left the band in '97 and was replaced by Muffs drummer Jim Laspesa. (Funny thing was, we didn't know Jim played bass! Our good pal from the LA Weekly, Dan Epstein, called me and said, "You gotta audition him. Trust me, he's great." Dan was spot-on. Jim did great.) I'd played all the bass on *Exploring Music*, as we were a trio at that point, and Nick Walusko and Darian Sahanaja (both from the Wondermints) produced and mixed the record. It was selling quite well...until Big Deal folded just before Christmas. To say we were disappointed would be an understatement.

In the year 2000, Rusty and I simultaneously released solo albums on EggBert Records. We did a short UK tour that November (including opening for the Wondermints in London) and then Baby Lemonade recorded one last album for Sympathy for the Record Industry, a song cycle we titled *The High Life Suite*.

◆◆◆

By 2001 I FELT PRETTY deflated and exhausted by the music business and enrolled in UCLA's certificate program for film scoring. I was on winter break when I got a phone call from David Fairweather. He said Arthur's case had been overturned on appeal and that he was being released! On December 21, the first day of winter, it got real when Arthur called. He was out and wanted to put the band back together. This time, he said, he wanted us to be Love full-time. I didn't mention that we had already stopped being Baby Lemonade after *The High Life Suite* was released.

We spent the spring of 2002 rehearsing and getting ready for the rigorous twenty-five-city European tour that awaited us in May. We did a warm-up show at Spaceland in Silverlake before that tour, and Arthur was even better than before he went to prison. After that successful tour we began to prepare for a set that would feature a string and horn ensemble, as we were planning to perform Love's magnum opus, *Forever Changes*, in its entirety. Early 2003 found us touring a lot with the Stockholm Strings and Horns and having heroes like Robyn Hitchcock, Graham Coxon, Nash Kato, and even Meg White sit in with us.

One day while Arthur was in Memphis visiting family, I got a call from Robyn Hitchcock. He was doing a show at Largo with Jon Brion and wanted to know if Baby Lemonade would pop down and play a few *Forever Changes* tunes with him. We couldn't get down there fast enough. (And somewhere Largo has a recording of that show!) Our UK management was working on a record deal for the new material we wrote with Arthur. After Snapper Records in London had released the Royal Festival Hall live show, legendary record producer John Leckie let it be known that he was down to produce the next Arthur Lee record. John Leckie?! We were beside ourselves since he's the guy who made Radiohead's *The Bends* and the Posies's *Dear 23*. We finished 2004 doing a US tour with the Zombies, which remains a real highlight of my life.

By 2005, things were receding. The new songs didn't seem to be much of a priority anymore. We did a couple of crappy shows in San Francisco at the Cafe du Nord as a warm-up to our upcoming summer UK/European tour—the one that Arthur didn't make. He missed the flight, and then the London bombings happened a week later. Arthur was ill and he hadn't told anyone. The day before the bombing, Rusty and I had beers with John Leckie at the Zodiac in Oxford. He still seemed keen to work with us if Arthur were "in the right state," but it was never to be. Sadly, Arthur was diagnosed with leukemia and passed away in August 2006.

In the fall of 2007, Baby Lemonade were hired to perform the entire *Sgt. Pepper's Lonely Hearts Club Band* album with the London Sinfonietta in Milan, Italy. The guest singers were Alex

Chilton, Robyn Hitchcock, Marianne Faithful, Beth Orton, Russell Mael, Badly Drawn Boy, and Jarvis Cocker. We were put up in a beautiful, old hotel for a week. Rehearsals were really fun and the show was a slice of heaven. Even a cranky Alex Chilton paid me a compliment on my guitar skills.

◆◆◆

FROM 2009 TO 2015, we only played shows with original Love guitarist, Johnny Echols, as Love Revisited. Then, in August of 2015 Baby Lemonade were asked to open for Rain Parade as part of a reunion band series at the Morgan-Wixson Theatre in Santa Monica. It felt great to play the songs again, especially to a sold-out audience. Baby Lemonade also entered into an agreement with New York–based Darla Records that year. They now carry our entire digital catalog, as well as hard copies of our "best of" CD.

We played another show for David Bash's International Pop Overthrow festival as a favor to him in 2018. And in March of 2020, Baby Lemonade opened for Love Revisited and the Forever Changes String and Horn Ensemble for the first time ever. Now there's talk of recording new music and playing more shows in the UK and Europe in 2021. Almost thirty years later and Baby Lemonade is definitely not slowing down.

Mike Randle *is the lead guitarist and cosinger/cosongwriter of LA power pop alchemists, Baby Lemonade, and also served as Arthur Lee's longest tenured lead guitarist (1993–2005). He is currently finishing his first book,* Singing Cowboy: A LOVE Guitarist's Diary of Adventures in King Arthur's Court. *Fourteen years after Arthur's passing, Mike and his Baby Lemonade bandmates continue to spread LOVE's music worldwide as LOVE Revisited.*

Marvelous

By Butch Walker

W E WERE THREE GUYS from a small town in north Georgia. It was the late eighties and we had everything and nothing; great families, shitty jobs. One thing was certain: we were getting out.

Cut to ten years later. A lot had happened on the way to achieving our rock dreams. Our heavy metal band moved to LA, signed record deals, swapped girlfriends, and lived off fifteen dollars a week. We played to just the bartender, slept with the bartender, and married the bartender. We played around the world and got exiled in China. There were breakups and divorces, near-death experiences, several van accidents, and street brawls. Bands changed, clothes changed, styles changed. And there we were.

Sometime around '97 we were back in Georgia when I had an idea for a side project. My best friend, bassist, and bandmate of ten years, Jayce Fincher, was having a baby with his wife, Chrystina (covocalist in our band at the time). I was in my mid-twenties and brimming with ideas fueled by post-divorce drive and venom. I couldn't slow down or wait for anyone. I had songs to record. So, I started something with Slug (aka Doug Mitchell), my other best friend and drummer for the past ten years.

We had no money, no backing, no future, really. But I had this one song in my back pocket. It was a little ditty about selling out and coming to terms with stardom (not that I knew what that was like). I was projecting like a motherfucker.

I'd recorded a bunch of demos on my digital sixteen-track tape machine in a rundown garage in East Atlanta where I rented a room from my buddy. We set up and recorded an album that sounded like a cross between the Knack, Raspberries, the Sweet—I don't know what. I loved this genre called power pop, although I didn't know that's what it was called. I just thought it was rock music played by guys with good hair. I had recently heard my older sister's boyfriend sing at a high school bonfire with his band. The first thing they played was a song called "She Sheila" by a band down the road in Atlanta called the Producers. It really hit me hard. The tempo, the chords, the melodies, the lyrics. The energy. It was everything I loved about the early eighties, all rolled into a tight, feather-haired, blue blazer-wearing package.

I played my new album for Jayce and he lost his mind when it got to the second song. I almost skipped that track because I thought it was "trying too hard to be a hit." He said, "That's it!" I said, "Whatever, sure," and didn't think much more about it.

One day I went to see my friend Steve Craig, a local DJ at the Atlanta alternative rock station 99X. Steve hosted a Sunday Night show called "Locals Only" that was pretty much only listened to by local musicians. I loved it and was determined to get this new project on that show. When I visited Steve in his cubicle, I handed him the ten-song CD-R with "The Marvelous 3" written on it. (A British singer and buddy named Ian Weber and I came up with the band name at Smith's Olde Bar over drinks one night.)

Steve played the first song and tapped his foot. He skipped to song two on the disc and played about forty-five seconds of it (the chorus comes in about twenty seconds after the song starts). I could see his wheels turning when he got through the chorus. Steve got up and said, "Follow me." He walked right into Leslie Fram's office, the station's program director, and said, "I'm sorry, but you have to hear this right now."

She put on the first song, tapped her feet, said it was good. Then she skipped to the second song. She hit stop after forty-five seconds (again) and said, "This is a smash hit song. Do you mind if I start playing it in regular rotation on the radio here?" I couldn't breathe. I was screaming inside. I remember saying, "Do you know how long I've been trying to get someone to listen to my music? I've been turned down by every record company and agent in the business. Please don't be pulling my leg here." Leslie looked at Steve. Steve looked at Leslie. Leslie looked at me and said, "Well, they're all about to offer you whatever you want."

That second song on the CD-R (sorry, it has a name—"Freak of the Week") started burning up the phones, the most requested song in Atlanta. It soon became a top-five hit on alt rock radio across the US. Soon I was getting offered blank checks from the same labels that said we looked funny with skinny ties, eyeliner, and tight black jeans (this was when JNCOs and dreads were popular). Suddenly they were flying us out to LA and NYC for fancy dinners and all that cliched shit. We loved it.

The *Hey! Album* was released by Elektra in 1998. There we were again, out of the van and back into a bus. The Marvelous 3 toured festivals and did pie-eating contests for radio station DJs with stupid names like "The Grinder" or "The Shocker." We filmed expensive videos, got free ugly clothes, and made our hair even weirder. It was everything we wanted and then…it just stopped happening.

Back in LA, we played a radio show at the Whisky (the same fucking place our metal band played its first show ever ten years before). I was rude on the mic that night. Drunk. Cocky. The radio station's program director said something like this to our label guy after we played: "They look like the Knack. They look ridiculous. We play bands that look more fashionable, like Korn." Why?

And just like that, it was over. That program director was the tastemaker for every alt rock station around the country. We played that Whisky show as a favor to the radio station and he ended up dropping our single from its airwaves. Every other station followed his lead. It was a long, steady fight to the bottom.

The Marvelous 3 made a second record for Elektra (*ReadySexGo*), but it was already over. Jayce, Slug, and I were burned out. We'd been playing together for fifteen years, never spending a day apart. And we were tired of all the "gimmes" and political trade-offs the music business expected of us.

We broke up shortly after our second album (they couldn't keep us in a record deal if we didn't exist). At the risk of sounding like a prick here, several bands came along a few years later wearing skinny ties and eyeliner. They said they were influenced by us and that they started playing instruments after seeing our live shows. That felt good. And horrible. But good. Would I trade it for anything in the world? Yes, the chance to do it again. It was that fun.

The Marvelous 3. We were five years too early. Fifteen years too late.

Grammy-nominated guitar-slinger, troublemaker, raconteur, producer, and Georgia boy, **Butch Walker** *is the writer behind dozens of songs with hooks that just seem to stick with you.* Rolling Stone *has called Walker "one of America's best singer-songwriters." He's penned choruses you can't help but sing along to for artists ranging from Frank Turner to Taylor Swift and produced massive rock records for Weezer, Fall Out Boy, as well as Green Days' latest hit album* Father of All Motherfuckers. *He is a teller of authentic stories of exploits, predicaments, and romance that are filled with optimism and a builder of albums with no boundaries.*

Love So Pure: Puffy AmiYumi Was Always Too Good for This World

By Andrea Warner

IN MID-2001, JAPANESE BAND Puffy AmiYumi released its North American debut, *Spike*. The title was, and is, perfect. It's satisfying to say: succinct, exact, winking but never precious. It's a word loaded with attitude and function, history and industrialization, and art and pop culture associations. It's a lot to shoulder for five letters, but spike's strange burden is also its power. It's an evocative word, and Puffy AmiYumi's *Spike* doesn't just embrace its title's myriad connotations, it embodies them.

Playful, thrilling, and unexpected, *Spike* isn't so much a cohesive narrative as it is a collection of joyful declarations and confident middle fingers. Puffy AmiYumi wasn't afraid of the critics naming and mapping its influences, and the band didn't care about categorization and genre delineations. Puffy AmiYumi wanted a sound that was familiar and wild and fun, and to make music they loved and share it with the world. What they got when they arrived in North America was a lot of music journalism at its worst: racist, sexist, gatekeeper coverage that often, even when "celebrating" the band, was rife with microaggressions and assumptions that Ami Onuki and Yumi Yoshimura, the two young Japanese women who fronted Puffy

AmiYumi, were the product of Svengali-type music producers and songwriters.

Puffy AmiYumi deserved better then, and they deserve better now. This is a brief look at what the band faced when they came to North America.

◆◆◆

AMI ONUKI AND YUMI Yoshimura were strangers when they were signed as teens to Sony Music in Japan. When they finally met, they bonded over their shared experiences. Onuki was working on a solo album with songwriter and producer Tamio Okuda (formerly of the Japanese rock band Unicorns), but meeting Yoshimura inspired Onuki to shelve the project in favor of cofounding a new act together. Okuda agreed to produce their debut and cowrote a number of songs, buoyant but barbed, raucous pop anchored by Onuki and Yoshimura's joyful harmonies. Okuda's collaborator, songwriter, and producer Andy Sturmer (formerly of the American pop band Jellyfish) came up with the band's name: Puffy.

Puffy's 1996 debut, *AmiYumi*, earned Puffy the 1996 Japan Record Award for Best New Artist, and launched Onuki and Yoshimura into the spotlight. Over the course of their first five years, Puffy released five albums. Onuki and Yoshimura worked with Okuda and Sturmer, who were foundational to Puffy's broad musical landscape. Together, they developed a deliberately varied sound for Puffy, experimenting with, to name a few, punk, surf rock, new wave, dance, electronic, disco, glam rock, techno, and, most definitively, power pop.

Spike was released in Japan in 2000 and North America in 2001 under the name Puffy AmiYumi (they added the AmiYumi to avoid a legal hassle with Sean "Puffy" Combs, as the rapper/

mogul was then known). Breaking into North America wasn't going to be easy, but Puffy AmiYumi brought with it an impressive fandom (thanks in part to their own TV show), their own toys and shoes, massive record sales (14 million by most published accounts), and a wildly successful back catalog of compelling songs. The US edition of *Spike* was a perfect showcase: frenetic and irresistible with song titles that were often their own works of art in parallel to the music, which unfolded like a wildly fascinating ride through the twentieth century. From the swing revival opener "Boogie Woogie No. 5" and the strutting tour-de-force "Shut Your Mouth, Honey" to the spaced out psychedelic rock of "Destruction Pancake" and the melodic power pop of "Love So Pure," *Spike* was track after track of controlled chaos.

But most of the media coverage of Puffy AmiYumi failed to clock *Spike* as subversive, even though the clue was right there in the name. *Spike* is an assertion, and everything about Puffy Ami-Yumi has always been deliberate. Calling the record *Spike* could have been a preemptive strike against North American media coverage. *Spike* could counteract the perceived softness of a pop band fronted by two young Japanese women. *Spike* could implicitly challenge the sexist and racist stereotypes facing young Japanese women, particularly in the music industry. *Spike* should have given pause to numerous North American critics and journalists to think about their unconscious bias, but it didn't. Even articles seemingly praising the band's music were awash in everything from references to "Hello Kitty" to infantilizing and/or sexualizing Onuki and Yoshimura as "cute," "yummy," and "doll-like."

Among the most questionable reviews of Puffy AmiYumi's *Spike* is from the *Globe and Mail*'s Robert Everett-Green. He gives the album three out of four stars and opens with "in the decorative arts, 'japanning' refers to a technique of covering any kind of object with a glossy, opaque varnish. Something similar has been going on for decades among Japanese pop musicians, who can make familiar Western genres sound impenetrably weird just by playing them straight." He briefly describes a couple songs and then concludes the next paragraph with "from the earnestly manic jungle-romp drumming to the nasal unison vocals in the language of Sei Shonagon [sic], this is japanning of the most entertaining kind."

There are several things to critique in Everett-Green's writing—"impenetrably weird just by playing them straight" because...they're Japanese?—but the most jarring is what's excerpted here and the metaphor he chose as a framework for the whole review: "japanning."

"Japanning" was the name Europeans gave to their process of imitating Asian forms of lacquering. This literally has its roots in colonialism. The writer thinks it's clever, but it's just racist, and it's further damaging to not acknowledge the roots of "japanning" in white supremacy while clumsily accusing Puffy AmiYumi of performing "Western" [re: white] music that was largely stolen and appropriated from Black and Indigenous artists.

It's almost impossible to know what Everett-Green means by "the nasal unison vocals in the language of Sei Shonagon [sic]." Even researching Sei Shōnagon—a Japanese author circa the year 1000 who began working at the age of fourteen in service to the Empress Consort Teishi; Japanese scholars apparently consider Sei Shōnagon's text the Pillow Book "a model of linguistic purity because it uses concise language and few Chinese words"[16]— doesn't resolve the sentence's key problem, which is Everett-Green. In trying to prove himself a lowkey authority on Japanese culture, he is centering himself at the expense of Puffy AmiYumi.

---

16 https://www.newworldencyclopedia.org/entry/Sei_Shonagon

In 2002, Puffy AmiYumi released their second North American album, *An Illustrated History*, a compilation of the band's hits from Japan. *Willamette Week* ran an interview with Onuki and Yoshimirua with the headline "Yummy Japanese Girl Pop" and the subhead "Don't look at us like that—they're Puffy AmiYumi, and they're here to be loved."

The article, written by Ben Munat, goes on to describe them as a "super-cute sugar-pop duo." Onuki and Yoshimura's quotes are humble and disarming throughout as they talk about their hopes that American audiences will give them a chance and how happy they are to be playing in the States, while the writer is doing what in dating terms can only be described as negging. Munat doesn't use Onuki and Yoshimura's last names, referring to them as Ami and Yumi throughout. He hypothesizes their influences, writing "a short list of stylistic landmarks might include ELO, Abba, the Who, the Beatles, the Beach Boys, the Jam, Motown…" to set up the following exchange:

> "'We just try to do something interesting and really fun,' explains Ami. So that's it.
>
> Now it's time for the inevitable invasion of America, where it remains to be seen whether kids will spend in the Puffy AmiYumi pop rummage sale. One stumbling block will certainly be that most of their lyrics are in Japanese. 'It may be difficult,' agrees Ami. 'Nonetheless, you will get the vibe of what we are singing about.'
>
> But when has anyone gone wrong by being cute, Japanese, and palatable? Forget not the cross-cultural superforce that is Hello Kitty."

Munat's editorializing within the piece—"so that's it" after Onuki speaks—is infuriating. But so, too, is reductively summarizing Puffy AmiYumi as "cute, Japanese, and palatable," not to mention the dehumanizing headline and subhead.

Puffy AmiYumi also encountered thinly veiled contempt by the media for their perceived lack of "authenticity," art's greatest gendered and/or racist dog whistle.

In 2002, the *LA Times* ran a feature called "Made in Japan" by Dean Kuipers, who begins his piece by describing Puffy AmiYumi as an "adorable bubblegum duo." He continues, "Given the fairly sustained mania over Britney, boy bands, and upbeat fluff in this country, could it be the right moment for the two to break out of their Japanese-only niche? Either way, these events would seem to mark the death of J-kitsch as an ironic statement. Goodbye, Hello Kitty."

The piece continues at length with Kuipers hypothesizing that "the end of irony" may "hurt" Puffy AmiYumi because their "brand of J-Pop is driven by honest stylistic tribute, but to American ears it may sound secondhand." He credits the duo as "stylists of the first order" before attributing their "carefully harvested sounds" to "studio wizards" Okuda and Sturmer. That praise is short-lived as Kuipers immediately declares the songs "only a backdrop" to the "signature vocal harmonies."

Kuipers eventually concludes that although Puffy AmiYumi will have to "find something original in their Japanese take on pop music or style," the duo was "stepping into friendly waters, with a young American radio public acclimated to singing stars and producer-driven clone bands. The playful, squeaky-clean image might go over with young girls in particular."

Because obviously, one: Puffy AmiYumi were just another "clone band," and two: young girls' interests are just not as discerning as, say, grown white men's. So, what does Kuipers hold up as having cultural value? Well, the "about" section of his website references his extensive writing on "radical movements and rock 'n' roll" and lists among his cover stories, "David Bowie, Neil Young, Iggy Pop, Smashing Pumpkins, Cypress Hill, the Rolling Stones, Marilyn Manson, and many others. As author and editor of the 1997 graphics/pop culture book *Ray Gun Out of Control*, he worked with contributors Bowie, REM's Michael Stipe, and cyberpunk writer William Gibson."[17]

Yes, *men* have cultural value and *male artists* hold the most cultural currency for Kuipers based on whose work he highlights in his own biography.

So, who gets to be authentic and original? Is it just the songwriters? Is Elton John just a puppet dancing on the hand of Bernie Taupin? Does it always come down to a hierarchical structure, and if it is a hierarchy, how come there are so many moving parts that always seem to specifically minimize and erase women, particularly racialized women, from their own bands?

In the case of Puffy AmiYumi, it didn't matter that Onuki and Yoshimura were often cocredited as songwriters. Okuda and Sturmer were the established musicians, the "wizards" behind the curtain of Puffy AmiYumi. Eventually even Okuda's contributions were minimized by North American media. A 2002 *SF Weekly* review of *An Illustrated History* reads, "It's obvious Puffy has a secret songwriting weapon: American Svengali and former Jellyfish drummer Andy Sturmer." In 2003, Sturmer was credited as the sole producer and cowrote the majority of songs on Puffy AmiYumi's North American release, *Nice.*—another stellar title with an important piece of punctuation—and Okuda wrote just one song.

Even Puffy AmiYumi's label made a point of talking about the importance of Onuki and Yoshimura's contributions as

17 http://www.deankuipersonline.com/about/

cowriters and artists who embodied the songs and brought them to the masses. The mythology of Puffy AmiYumi as the brainchild of two men was a media creation. There are countless additional examples of the ways in which North American music journalists—particularly straight, white men—failed Puffy AmiYumi. They exoticized, objectified, stereotyped, sexualized, infantilized, minimized, and othered Onuki and Yoshimura, consciously or subconsciously, in an attempt to invalidate the pair as artists, musicians, and people. It's impossible to quantifiably measure the effects of this kind of media coverage on Onuki or Yoshimura, or know exactly how damaging it was to Puffy AmiYumi as a whole.

The band's last North American studio release was 2009's *Bring It*, while the last Japanese studio release was 2011's *Thank You*. But Puffy AmiYumi are still together. The band has released several compilation albums, EPs, and singles since 2011. And, after a decade away, Puffy AmiYumi finally returned to the US on tour in 2017. In an interview that same year with J-Generation, Onuki reflected on her relationship with Yoshimura and what they've built together: "Only we know [how] it feels to be Puffy AmiYumi—in a way no one else in the world, even our families, would understand."

This is key. Okuda and Sturmer are important to Puffy AmiYumi, but there wouldn't even be a Puffy AmiYumi without Onuki and Yoshimura. These two artists deserve to be written back into their own band's history. It's on music journalists and critics to hold ourselves accountable for the harm we have caused.

Andrea Warner *writes and talks. She is the author of* Buffy Sainte-Marie: The Authorized Biography *and* We Oughta Know: How Four Women Ruled the '90s and Changed Canadian Music. *Andrea has cohosted* Pop This! *podcast since 2015 and is a panelist on CBC's Pop Chat podcast. She's a settler who was born and raised in Vancouver on the unceded traditional territories of the Musqueam, Squamish, and Tsleil-Waututh First Nations. @_ AndreaWarner*

Ode on a Rickenbacker

By Rex Broome

Mine's a Rickenbacker 610-12. She's a semi-rare example of the little-remembered downscale cousin of the compact hardbody 620 probably best known for hanging off of Tom Petty's shoulders on the iconic cover of *Damn The Torpedoes*. She lacks the fancy binding and the sexy triangle fretboard inlays. She's basic black, and she's battered and covered with stickers in a punk-rock way that a fussy collector would never countenance. Her molecules have spent more time in contact with my own than those of any other object or person. She's my lifelong companion. We've been through a lot together and I do adore her.

I'm not here to rhapsodize about Rickenbackers, exactly. Lord knows there are easier guitars to tune and play. I love mine (and her ersatz sister, a blonde 330-6 with black hardware I scored in the greatest eBay coup ever), but that's down to its near-genetic connection to my entire playing history and the fact that I don't "collect" guitars and haven't traded out my primary axe in over thirty years. She's simply a part of me, and we have the same kind of occasionally fraught relationship as any long-married couple. All in the name of "that sound."

"What sound?" you ask. That's a matter for debate. Ricks are often said to only do one thing—"chime," in record-review parlance—but do it well. I'm not convinced they're quite so limited. Players like Paul Weller in the early Jam and Brix Smith in the Fall managed to wring plenty of garage-y clang out of their 330s, and the Smithereens based their entire sound on Ricks with crunch, abetted by the strategy of down tuning them. Ride coinvented shoegaze by making theirs howl. My own affinity for the electric twelve-string sound comes as much from the spooky stuff the Church's Marty Willson-Piper and the early unschooled Peter Buck did with them, and the more out-there jazz-raga experiments of Roger McGuinn on the Byrds' mid-period records like *5-D* and *Notorious Byrd Brothers* as from anything purely "pop." Besides which, if you're going to knock unvaried guitar sounds, you'll need to throw out your Ramones and Zeppelin records along with your Icicle Works. Jangly consistency is not necessarily the hobgoblin of small-minded guitar tones.

But we're here between the covers of a book on power pop, and the mystery in front of us is that of the Rickenbacker as "the" guitar of choice for the genre. And the truth is, they're more figurehead than favored axe. They're generally a tool brought to bear when that particular jangle tone is needed, often in the studio. On stage I tend to see pop bands bring out their usually pristine Rick twelves for the one or two especially chime-y numbers while relying on well-worn Telecasters and Gibson-related hollow-bodies for the bulk of their sets. And that makes sense: those guitars are a lot more no-nonsense for gigging musicians and sound great on record, too. Everything about a Tele is perfect, and it most assuredly does more than one thing while the Rick twelve in practice is often more akin to the Theremin or the Mellotron: a shorthand sound to signify an influence or an era.

So how, and, maybe more importantly, when, did Rickenbackers become the iconic power pop guitar? My anecdotal conclusion is that it was 1997. That's when Rhino Records released the *Poptopia! Power Pop Classics* trio of CDs covering the seventies, eighties, and nineties eras of the genre and arguably codified its specifics for a wider audience. And right there on the cover art for the seventies installment, designed by Hugh Brown with acknowledged apologies to Roy Lichtenstein, is an instantly recognizable detail of the pickguard and literally copyrighted "R" tailpiece of a Fireglo 330.

And it's really a bravura bit of work. Its pop-art styling nods both to the name of the genre and the aesthetic largely established by Jordan Oakes' *Yellow Pills* to frame it. And the Rick looks…just right. Switch it out for a Strat and you'd have something not too different from a clip-art flyer for a "Rock and Roll Fundraiser" at your kid's nursery school. As it stands, the angles of the guitar, described with a few simple swooping lines and filled in solely with vibrant primary colors, speak volumes.

Personally, though, I don't think they speak to power pop itself as it stood at the time of the compilation's release, which is why I'm positing that single image as the watershed moment. It's both a strength and albatross of the genre that it has, as the decade-based titles of the *Poptopia* series' installments indicate, arisen in different forms in ways that other genres have not. But the bands collected on the seventies volume alone—Badfinger, Big Star, Cheap Trick, and Flamin' Groovies alongside a few slightly more obscure touchstones—don't immediately conjure images of lipstick pickups and cat's-eye f-holes. Project yourself forward to the new wave–adjacent resurgence in the eighties and that's Strat city, baby. Jump to the nineties and you're looking at an array of hipster-friendly junk-shop guitars.

Retro chic hadn't yet set in because the music was still, miraculously, pushing forward with its most basic of building blocks. You'd see Ricks in power pop occasionally—hey there, Plimsouls!—but they were largely viewed as upscale college-rock axes for a lot of that time. I can even recall some players speaking with pride that they'd used Danoelectro, Fender, and even Daisy Rock twelve-strings on their records rather than a ritzy Rickenbacker International Corporation product.

And then, around the turn of the century, something happened that's an essay or a book of its own: the final and inevitable fragmenting of the rock and roll canon (redirect to Limp Bizkit, Napster panic, the well-earned collapse of the music industry, etc.), which sapped the very last bit of now-ness—which is not to say quality or potentially brilliant inventiveness, just simple cultural currency—out of the form, more or less forever.

And that basically means we've all been doing some version of the Beatles ever since. So hey, Rickenbackers!

"Now hold up there, Broome," you may say. "Aren't Ricks more of a Byrds thing?" Sure. And plenty of power pop purveyors revere the Byrds, the Beach Boys, the Kinks, and the other sixties originators mightily. But reductivism has taken hold and too many of the folks struggling to be heard in the post-rock age fall back on the tropes of the Fabs, who are, to all intents and purposes, the only band of the era known—often in encyclopedic depth and to the exclusion of any peers shy of the Stones—by people born after, say, 1985. I now teach rock and roll to their kids for my "day job," so trust me on this.

I must admit, it's mildly frustrating that modern power pop leans into barely redressed Beatlemania with the Rickenbacker as emblem. Fair enough, on the face of it: John Lennon's 325 will always be the best-known specimen, and Harrison's twelve-string experiments got McGuinn thinking electric. And that might be why Ricks are seen as British Invasion signifiers despite having been glued together by hand in Santa Ana for more than half a century. But history's written by the winners, and modern rock orthodoxy was conquered by the Beatles, and since they're even more prototypical of power pop than rock at large, here we are.

I'm not going to decry retro-ism too ferociously, nor is my beloved and long-suffering 610 going into mothballs. In fact, I'm proud to have shared stages with and been responsible alongside Christina Bulbenko and Big Stir Records for releasing music by such Rick-twelve devotees as Peter Watts (Spygenius) and John Ashfield (the Bobbleheads), who still put the songwriting before the nostalgia, and put as much into doing what the *Revolver*-era Beatles and the *5-D* Byrds—or, hell, the *In The City* Jam and the REM of *Murmur*—did in pushing the rock and roll idiom forward as the particular sounds they committed to vinyl. Neither hooks nor jangle need to be rote or boring.

If it sounds like I'm saying that a Rick twelve can be just as punk rock as Pete Shelley's busted-ass Starway…I am. I also love power pop at its best enough that I'm fully content with the Rickenbacker serving as its avatar. If there's a bit of tension between those two viewpoints, that's the nature of the beast. Just like the microtonal variances between the paired strings that mean the damn thing's never gonna really be in tune. That tension is where the beauty lies.

Rex Broome *is the cofounder (with Christina Bulbenko) of Big Stir Records and a singer/guitarist/songwriter with LA band the Armoires (also with Bulbenko). Beyond its physical and digital releases of records for key artists on the global pop rock scene, Big Stir is a multimedia entity dedicated to musical community building, also producing live shows in the US and UK, publishing a magazine, and curating a weekly Singles Series.*